Dear Lisa

We, I hope, are on the right path for big accomplishment

Warmest & greeting

Mark D

10/23/2013

TRANSCENDENCE

SAVING US FROM OURSELVES

NEW YORK

TRANSCENDENCE

SAVING US FROM OURSELVES

Navin Doshi

Ithaca Press
3 Kimberly Drive, Suite B
Dryden, New York 13053 USA
www.IthacaPress.com

Cover Design   Gary Hoffman
Book Design   Gary Hoffman

Manufactured in the United States of America

9 8 7 6 5 4 3 2 1

Library of Congress Cataloging-in-Data Available
Doshi/Navin   Philosophy, Economics/Eastern Philosophy/
India/ Self Help/Enlightenment/

ISBN 978-0-9815116-3-4

First Edition

Printed in the United States of America

www.NavinDoshi.com

Accolades

"In this wonderful book, Navin Doshi raises some of the questions that have puzzled people of all races and creeds since ancient times. The author combines the wisdom of Indian scriptures with the lessons of modern science, a task that he is well qualified to accomplish. Doshi demonstrates that lasting happiness is possible only when we learn how to protect ourselves from the self-centered demands of our minds. *Saving Us from Ourselves* is indeed a great thought by itself."

Ravi Batra, author of *Greenspan's Fraud,* a New York Times bestseller

"*Saving Us from Ourselve*s is the work of a thinker who is also a doer. Doshi, a reflecting entrepreneur from the East who succeeded in the West, is well aware of the hazards of self-centered living. Through his insightful aphorisms, the fruit of a lifetime of observation and experience, and by way of some delightful equations, the book seeks to summarize wisdom for the 21st century."

Rajmohan Gandhi

Author's note: Rajmohan Gandhi is a writer and former member of the Indian Parliament, and the grandson of Mahatma Gandhi and Rajgopalachari, the first Governor of India.

"Navin H. Doshi, a self-described student of life, confronts the greatest problems of our world today, including war, poverty, hatred, selfishness, and the corrosion of power and greed. He asks, 'Is transcendence possible from self-centeredness to selflessness, from intermittent, sporadic, finite happiness to a more stable state of being?' In the chapters that follow, Mr. Doshi answers this profound question. He presents an analysis of the current state of the world, along with his proposal to 'engender a peaceful and productive relationship with Nature.' Using his lifetime of studies in science, economics, and philosophy, along with the wisdom of Samskara from India, he believes that his 'path will lead all humanity to a state of peace and fulfillment.' In this study, many readers will find an approach to truth that they rarely, if ever, have experienced. *Saving Us from Ourselves* offers a unique and profound vision of reality that is richly rewarding and well worth careful study. Mr. Doshi reveals a path for personal transformation, one that holds immense potential for addressing today's problems and for stimulating creative solutions."

Michael E. Engh, S.J., Dean of Bellarmine College of Liberal Arts,
Loyola Marymount University, Los Angeles, California, USA

"I am really moved by your last paragraph on 'Gandhi's Spirituality.' 'You may change the path to go around the obstacles, so long as the direction is toward the mountaintop, where all paths meet.' Beautiful and enchanting."

A. P. J. Abdul Kalam, former President of India
Author's note: The President's comments were made about my article on Gandhi's spirituality
(See page 90, Ch. 4).

"In his book *Saving Us from Ourselves*, Navin Doshi has masterfully articulated the role and interaction of our somatic, psychic, and spiritual selves with Nature. Capitalizing on his life experiences in India and the United States, he has demonstrated with great skill that the wisdom and life principles contained in Indian scripture such as the Vedas and the Gita, which at times appear to be contradictory, are actually complementary to Western culture and thought. Mr. Doshi makes a compelling argument that for the sake of real happiness and fulfillment one must go beyond the physical and psychological selves and resolve duality to achieve wholeness. After reading his book, I have developed a great appreciation of his contributions to the well-being of society."

Vijay K. Dhir, Distinguished Professor and Dean,
Henry Samueli School of Engineering and Applied Science, UCLA

"This very readable book describes a philosophy of life informed by traditional wisdom and direct experience. Grounded in knowledge of the Vedas and reflections on a lifetime of experience, Navin Doshi suggests that transcendence from our somatic self and our mental capacities aspires to a sense of spirituality. In the journey to fulfillment, all aspects of being human need cultivation and care, moving toward a cosmic order that harmonizes self and Nature. The book includes a gentle introduction to key concepts of Indian philosophy and modern science, as well as a useful glossary of Sanskrit terms."

Christopher Key Chapple, Associate Academic Vice President and Professor of Theological Studies,
Loyola Marymount University, Los Angeles

"The author takes a spiritual view of the subject and brings to it very unusual insight. Science obviously does not have answers to all our questions, but it does have a legitimate regulative role in the pursuit of knowledge."

Bhikhu Parekh, F.B.A.
Author's note: Dr. Parekh, former Vice Chancellor of M.S. University of Baroda, is a member of the House of
Lords, U.K.

"As advances are made in the sciences, psychology, and metaphysics, we see analogous patterns emerge. Navin Doshi has utilized his experiences in India in his youth and those later in the USA to make important observations on human behavior and draw illuminating conclusions. His knowledge of India's traditions and his experiences in the West uniquely enable him to discuss how the various dimensions of human experience are equally important and necessary for the evolution of human development. In *Saving Us from Ourselves*, he blends the teachings of authors—ancient and modern—to convey how human civilization and cultural growth are strongly influenced by our thoughts and actions, and can lead to personal transformation."

Distinguished Professor C. R. Vishwanathan, UCLA, and former Chairman,
University of California Statewide Academic Senate

"As a co-worker for many years at TRW Defense and Space, I have observed Navin's successes as an engineer and in personal wealth building. Relating his experiences in the fields of science and economics to ancient Indian philosophy, his concern for the environment, education, and in general a better life for every one of us should be a source of inspiration to younger generations. The book connects the themes of films with its content, encouraging the reader to better understand the subject matter."

Dr. Pravin Bhuta, Retired Manager, Advanced Technology, TRW Defense and Space

"Western societies are well-known for their tendency toward dualisms of many sorts: good vs. evil, truth and fiction, and so on. The traditions of India offer an important alternative, and, *in Saving Us from Ourselves,* Navin Doshi has provided an introduction to Indic wisdom and the concept of Samskara in a work that touches on psychology, quantum physics, economics, and religion. The body is capable of Samskaric transformation, discerning a middle path between suppression and out-of-control growth. Doshi is on a 'search for solutions and opportunities,' and *Saving Us from Ourselves* is a window on his fruitful path."

Robert A. Hurteau, Ph.D., Director, Center for Religion and Spirituality,
Loyola Marymount University, Los Angeles

"With modernity's inordinate transgression on tradition in our turbulent times, philosophers and historians inevitably wrestled to produce a new human equation. In this insightful book on how the human race may save itself from itself, Navin Doshi uses his life's experience to provide an interaction of science and humanities, philosophy and economics, nature and human intrusion. In the end, drawing on the Indian tradition, he provides a *solution,* with charts and diagrams, for the successful *evolutionary process* of a human being dealing with the three 'autonomous' domains—somatic, psychic and spiritual—connecting one domain with the next. Very commendable, indeed."

D. R. SarDesai, Emeritus Professor of History, UCLA

"We are so impressed with the interdisciplinary nature of the book. [T]he content is original in its approach."

Kumar and Shela Patel, Author's note: Kumar Patel is the inventor of the CO2 laser, and former Vice Chancellor of Research, UCLA. He is currently a CEO of Pranalytica.

"I am absolutely amazed at the depth you bring to India's culture and its symbolism with Nature. There are books written about Man, Nature, and God, but none that I know of about understanding how we are each divine and have a role in life. I was intrigued about the fact that 'events occur in clusters,' such as the autos on freeways and blood clots in the body...Thank you for providing such an impact with your visit and your book to the youth in our community."

Mayur Patel, Structural Engineer, F-35, Northrop Grumman Corporation

"*Saving Us from Ourselves* is an intellectual quest for meaning and unity of existence, and for enduring peace and happiness. Drawing upon the wisdom of Indic traditions and his own experiences, Navin Doshi provides an insightful and thought-provoking analysis of contemporary problems, and suggests that the remedy may be in the dissolution of all ego and identity—characteristic of a saint. It is only then that one may experience lasting peace within oneself, a sense of unity with others, and harmony with Nature."

Tara Sethia, Professor of History and Director of the Ahimsa Center, California State Polytechnic University, Pomona

"It is rare to find an individual who brings together valuable ideas from the East and the West, from philosophy and science, from economics and investment, and from ethics and psychology. Navin Doshi is that rare modern thinker who presents such a synthesis in a careful and comprehensive vision that engages ancient wisdom for addressing the challenges we face in modern times. The style of his work reminds me of the sacred Sanskrit classic from ancient India, the Bhagavad Gîtå.

Its work synthesizes many systems of thought but it also possesses an ultimate focus, which could be framed in his own simple but eloquent words: 'Ultimately, love binds all living creatures together.' Until we can know these profound words of Navin Doshi, humanity will never truly experience its intimate relationship with the Divine."

Graham M. Schweig, Ph.D., Professor of Religion and Director of Indic Studies Program, Christopher Newport University, Author-Translator, *Bhagavad Gītā: The Beloved Lord's Secret Love Song.*

"Reading Navin H.Doshi's *Saving Us from Ourselves* delivers in grand style the rare extraordinary experience and treat of subject matter dealing with education, philosophy, spirituality, and most importantly everyday common sense, never before issued in any other reading material in my lifetime. The inner benefits and wisdom I have received from this most talented author via this phenomenally precious book represents an enormous treasure for all generations yet to come. Thank you, Navin for "saving us."

Robert L. Friedman, Former President of AMC International, a film production and Entertainment Group, a member of the Academy and a voting member for Oscar selection

"Nothing is more important in our globalized world than to bridge the long-standing divides that have caused humanity so much grief: between East and West, science and religion, reason and belief, faith and fact, physical and spiritual. Navin Doshi, a man at home in many worlds, has bravely attempted to construct the necessary links, and he has done so in convincing, easy-to-understand language. Drawing on sources as old as the Vedas, and as contemporary as particle physics— not to mention "Forrest Gump"—he points us inward to consciousness, where we can find the needed resources to fix our self-created problems."

Philip Goldberg, author of *Roadsigns on the Spiritual Path* and Director of the Forge Guild of Spiritual Leaders.

CONTENTS

Acknowledgements

Thank you to my dear ones and good friends for helping to bring this book to fruition.

Dedication

This book is dedicated to all the Sages and Scholars of Ancient Indian Philosophy, from the past to the present.

Preface

Since the days of Marco Polo, there has been a fascination with all things from the East. East/West comparisons go well beyond the cultural and probe deeply into the very fabric of the human mind. But in fact the Eastern and Western minds are essentially the same except in cultural lexis, itself a superficial distinction. Maps of the human mind and the striving for equanimity and selflessness are never as exactly and fully charted as they are in Eastern thought, which legitimize doubt and self-examination. Why then do the comparisons of the two minds and two fundamental approaches to life continue to fuel as much scholarship and interest as they do? Perhaps it is because the essential problems of life remain unsolved, unresolved, and essentially unexamined by other than scholars, clerics, and enlightened human beings. Eastern maps deserve close consideration because they have emerged from minds that were born of centuries of self-reflection. When asked, J. Krishnamurti said that perhaps because of the climate, living outdoors, and from lack of interest in materialism, the Eastern mind developed differently and looked inward.

Expertly veiled as a familial memoir, *Savings Us from Ourselves*, replete with contemporary stories and vivid narrative pictures, is a cultured intellectual approach to understanding what has eluded the intellect since humanity reflected on its essential problems of living. What saves this paradox is that the author speaks from the high ground of perception and draws the reader up to the threshold of insight. What has eluded the intellect is what gave rise to *Samskara*, the unifying, holistic, and non-dualistic approach to life.

Navin Doshi offers much to contemplate in this book: the way to apprehend the profound is by contemplation—having an insight that is original—and moving beyond the words. His scientific approach moves from reasoned thought to reasoned thought with the quick perception of an observer trained to be concerned with the quality of his own observation.

When reading about serious matters of life and living, readers must be aware that the words on the page are illustrations of things and events in life, and be careful not to regard them with the unwarranted respect that bestows wholly abstract concepts with reality, as if standing alone and consequently unconnected with reality. Gratuitous reverence is often given philosophical and religious language if the words are foreign and removed enough from our common usage. It is what they point to that is of importance, but too often we obsess over the word-finger that points and do not attend to whatever it represents or is directing us to. Doshi points to a transcendent spontaneity of life that is beyond language. A *Mahayana* sutra reads, "The truth was never preached by the Buddha, seeing that you have to realize it within yourself." With contemporary style, Doshi makes it obvious that truth is seen by the unconditioned mind, one that has transcended all paths by traveling all paths and going beyond all descriptions. The abandonment of ourselves is our salvation, and Doshi, with affection for the human predicament, shows that to be the highest expression of love.

R. E. Mark Lee, Executive Director
Krishnamurti Foundation of America

Foreword

Currently, we are undergoing tremendous movements of separateness all around the world: global warming, terrorism, the breakdown of capitalism and democracy, the breakdown of liberal education, just to name a few. I think that much of the malaise that we see around us is due to one major conflict, that between our own materialist tendencies and spiritual tendencies. This is augmented by the paradigm battle that we are witnessing between science and spirituality.

Fortunately, although movements of separateness are creating an ever-widening abyss, concomitantly there are bridge builders. The book you are holding is by such a bridge builder Navin Doshi. Doshi is originally from India but has lived in America most of his life. So in a sense he has already built a bridge between the spiritual East and the material West in his own life. No doubt his life experiences have made a great contribution to the bridge-building ideas he shares with you in this book.

His main idea is this: The human being consists of three domains: the external physical body or soma, the internal psyche, and the transcending spirit. Naturally, our consciousness identifies with the conditioned patterns of each domain giving us three major self identities: the somatic self, the psychic self, and the unconditioned philosophical self. He says that there is a fourfold-ness in our nature: two, genetics and the physical body arising from the somatic self, the other two are intuition and the intellect arising from the psychic self. When we create society, we create it maintaining the same fourfold-ness. Thus he comes to the conclusion that much is gained by looking at our social phenomena in a fourfold way. Ultimately, of course, there has to be balance and harmony among the components.

In this way, a Doshi economics is formulated by finding four components in the field of economics corresponding to the genetic, the physical body, the intuitive mind and the intellect. Doshi postulates that these four components of economics are: the economic growth rate as measured by GDP, the unemployment rate, the inflation rate, and the interest rate. Doshi's economic remedy then is straightforward: establish balance and harmony between the four components.

If you are not a strict materialist and are willing to suspend your disbelief about mind and body coexisting with a transcending consciousness, a model that a quantum-based science within consciousness supports anyway, then you will enjoy this book and will find much to think about here. I recommend *Saving us from Ourselves* highly.

Amit Goswami
Professor emeritus of Physics, University of Oregon,
and the author of *The Self-Aware Universe, God is not Dead*,
and *Creative Evolution*.

Summary

The book title raises the question: who are we saving, and from whom?

We long to escape from our mental conditioning and fears; from a mundane existence; from endless repetitive behavior, like that of habitual gamblers or alcoholics; and from the corrosion of power and greed. Is transcendence possible from self-centeredness to selflessness, from intermittent, sporadic, finite happiness to a more stable state of being?

I have been a lifelong student of science, economics, philosophy, and life itself. This book is an account of my travels and studies, a travelogue of sorts, concerned with human life, both individual and societal, and its relationship with Nature. My journeys have taken me from East to West, from past to present. My focus, though, has largely been here and now, bringing me face to face with the crises of contemporary life—greed, fundamentalism, and the destruction of the human habitat—prompting a search for solutions and opportunities.

Problems, solutions and opportunities result from the dynamics of human relationships, internal and external. How can our relationships be optimized, made holistic and productive, rather than broken and destructive? To find right pathways and effective mechanisms to cultivate our somatic and psychic selves and to engender a peaceful and productive relationship with Nature is at the heart of this book.

The path I am proposing, using the Indian wisdom of Samskara effective in the ancient past, could be adopted in the current troubled times by all of us, the whole of humanity, for peace and fulfillment.

Samskara is the harnessing of spontaneous physical impulses and re-flexes within the somatic self. It also includes the integration of opposites through the experience of the senses and the nervous system of the body, key concepts of Eastern wisdom. The wisdom of Samskara is everywhere and in all traditions.

Cultural evolution has given us the tools of technology with which to become more knowledgeable about our physical bodies and Nature. However, progress in internal growth, of the psyche, seems slow. How do we accelerate this process?

Our value system needs changing to continuous education at all levels, without compromising individual freedom of choice. Free enterprise seems the most natural economic system. However, money and power over others ought not to be the ultimate goal of life. As Professor Ravi Batra has cited in his many books, CEOs need alternate motivation other than money. It is not necessary for a CEO to make hundreds of times more money than the average employee. There are plenty of examples recently, as with Enron or World Com, that show how easily corruption can spread.

John F. Kennedy's profound statement, "Ask not what your country can do for you, but what you can do for your country," can become the mantra of the transformed soul, one that will show the path to transformation from a self-centered individual to a selfless being, helping others.

Liberty and the freedom to choose are sacred, and must never be violated. Historically, fanaticism of beliefs and traditions feeds on ignorance and stifles intellectual pursuits. There are many examples like in China, Russia, and Germany where millions of people died. In these examples there was a spontaneous transformation due to the fear caused by a few communists or Nazis. Germans became Nazis because the silent majority did not protest, probably due to fear and transformed themselves just as it happens in an optical laser, where the transformation of photons occurs spontaneously, causing them to become "obedient" and conform like soldiers into a fine, non-diverging beam of light of a single color.

A gradual transformation within that comes by choice, a transformation that brings compassion and charity and a desire to transcend to a higher state of being is certainly preferred over an obedient instantaneous mindless laser-like, and forced, transformation of any kind.

This is where we must take a step back and look at our past. Going back tens of thousands of years, we see our oldest great, great, great grandparents originating in Ethiopia. The African tribes of Homo sapiens migrated to India, Java and to Australia, and central Asia, then moved to the west to Europe, and east to China, Alaska and finally to the Americas. Ever since then, we have been connected in some shape or form. And with today's technology of the Internet, cell phones and GPS systems, we are more connected than ever.

Humanity is now, more than ever before, transcending from individual consciousness, and moving toward a unified consciousness. This is all part of evolution within and evolution without. And now, we need to evolve more and faster within, that is, in the psychological domain. This is where the wisdom of scholars, saints and philosophers is indispensable to us.

Among changes that could preserve humanity are:

• the development of robust somatic and psychic selves that will help us to transcend and remove the fear of death;

• the understanding that good and evil are a pair of opposites that cannot be separated, that evil is the raw material for good;

• a "superconducting economy," where resistance to the flow of money is insignificant, and the misery index is close to zero because each able-bodied person is employed and the needs of the somatic self are satisfied;

• good training, education, and the harnessing of somatic desires to control population growth.

Chapter 1 examines the total human self and its interaction with Nature. Up close, we see that the total human self has within it three selves or domains, each one equal and autonomous—the somatic self, consisting of the body and genetics; the psychic self, consisting of intuition and intellect; and the self beyond—integrated, balanced and harmonized—also known as the spiritual self. These domains are layered, like an onion bulb, with further sub-layers. The regression and mixing of the selves is the first cause of problems and crises, along with the exploitative relationship of man with Nature.

In Chapter 2, the somatic self is examined, including a pre-psychic component that can be trained. The question is explored, how can the somatic self be made Samskaric?

The greatest contribution of Indian civilization to humanity is, according to some scholars, psychology. Chapter 3 concerns the psychic self and its two aspects, intuition and intellect. How can the psychic self be fully understood if priority is given to intellect and rationality at the cost of intuition, as the modern Western world seems to be doing? Only when the psychic self is well-balanced, functioning at both intuitive and intellectual levels in harmony, can it function productively, maintaining a proper relationship with the other selves and Nature.

The relation of the total human self, and autonomously the somatic and psychic selves with Nature, is all-important. How can a holistic, friendly, productive and peaceful relationship be formed? How did a destructive, domination-oriented relationship between man and Nature come about? What are the basic factors, at the level of the somatic and psychic selves, that need to be studied and cultivated—and how?

Mind (psyche) and matter (brain), atom and Atman (soul), particle and wave, order and chaos, and information and the initial condition of an order are discussed in Chapter 4. Well thought out processes are proposed, based on the author's interpretation of old scriptures and modern science. Clustering, non-judgmental autonomy, the 80/20 rule, sub-ration, and evolution are looked at, and the relationship of these processes to the living space of multiple dimensions and their boundaries. How can harmony and the direction toward the mountaintop be achieved through sub-ration and evolution, if the pathway of Samskara is accepted?

Issues of clustering, harmonies, the complementarity of two opposites, and balance are presented in Chapter 5. One of my original contributions to this book is on the clustering of the four fundamental elements of the total human self and their connection to any field of human endeavor and processes in society, nations, and Nature. These connections are explored in Tables 1 to 5.

Bridge building and patchwork coexistence are explored in Chapter 6. Transcendence from the rigidity and confinement of religion to the openness of spirituality is looked at. Both the tools of reductionism and integration are necessary for harmony and transcendence toward unity. Patchwork coexistence fosters peaceful relationships, allowing traditions to flourish without interference.

In Chapter 7, our journey culminates at the point where the unity of life might begin. How can human life be harmonized both internally and externally? Rupert Sheldrake speaks of the morphic field where what is learned by one individual of a species is made available to another member of the species in a distant part of the globe, without direct contact. What is the root of such unity of knowledge within a morphic field? How can our selves be so cultivated, educated, made Samskaric, to enter and enlarge such a field?

Scientists have demonstrated how an individual photon particle changes into a light wave, occupying a continuum of space and time. How does a self, as an analog, change from a self-centered "particle" into a universal self, like a "wave"? How do we transcend from one domain to another?

To culminate has another dimension—to end. Is death the end? What is its relationship with our moving on to another domain or realm of existence? Is it necessary to die philosophically in order to move on from one domain, like the somatic self, to another domain, like the psychic self? And then on to the spiritual self. What does it mean to die philosophically, and not just physically? The final chapter discusses, in short, the why, what and how of the internal unity of all life. Matters of inward and outward expansion and meditation described by J. Krishnamurti are also presented in this last chapter.

For the convenience of readers, a section at the end of Chapter 7, "Vision at a Glance through Aphorisms," gives the gist of my perceptions and vision of life.

Short appendices follow: a comparison of Darwin's theory of evolution with an ancient prophecy; Will Durant's view on human progress and Shankara's philosophy; synopses of Western films that reflect some of the premises of this book; insights from the book *The Celestine Prophecy*; and a discussion on mass human psychology and the laws of Nature.

Whispers

The man whispered, "God, speak to me,"
and a meadowlark sang.
But the man did not hear.

So the man yelled, "God, speak to me,"
and the thunder rolled across the sky.
But the man did not listen.

The man looked around and said, "God, let me see you,"
and a star shone brightly.
But the man did not see.

And the man shouted, "God, show me a miracle,"
and a life was born.
But the man did not notice.

So the man cried out in despair, "Touch me God, and let me
know you are here,"
whereupon God reached down and touched the man.
But the man brushed the butterfly away and walked on.

I found this to be a great reminder that God is always around us
in the little and simple things that we take for granted... even in
our electronic age.
So I would like to add one more:

The man cried, "God, I need your help,"
and an e-mail arrived reaching out with good news and encour-
agement.
But the man deleted it and continued crying.

Don't miss out on a blessing because it isn't packaged the way
that you expect.

—*From an unknown source*

Chapter 1
Of a Pilgrimage and Pathways

This book is about *Samskara* and much more. Instead of defining the term, let me share developments in my own life that gave me an intimate understanding of the unfolding of its meaning. An even more intimate experience was the very process of discovering something that I came later to know as *Samskara*. It could have been present in the marrow of my bones, in my genes, inherited from my parents, but it was through the idealism of my teachers and growing up during India's freedom movement and finally earning *Samskara* by my own efforts that I found the most satisfying. I was also influenced by the idealism I saw in some of the Western films I was exposed to during my young years. In fact, that was one reason I came to America, along with the opportunity for higher education.

I have, for several decades, felt a strong need to understand myself and the world in which I live with my fellow human beings. I was curious to know how and why some people succeed and some do not. To be of help to the latter was also a need for me, as strong as my need to be one of the former. Some might say that these impulses are part of my congenital nature. I neither dispute nor confirm that view. I consider myself a lifelong student of life, and I do not wish to miss out on the joy of being just that. I have neither been expelled nor graduated from the school of life.

The most decisive force that compelled me to pen my writings is my daughter, Sonya. On December 12, 2001, my 65th birthday, Sonya gave me a lovely gift, and asked, as only a daughter can, for a gift in return. Her gift was a journal with fresh, smooth sheets of paper. The return gift that she wanted was spelled out in her own words in the front of the journal: "To My Dear Dad, I hope you will use this journal to record some of your experiences as a person, a son, an Indian, an immigrant, a father, and of course, as a 'student of life.'" She went on to tell me that I have a vivid memory and many great stories, and she would love to have at least some written down for her to enjoy and "to look back upon in future years." "Who knows," Sonya wondered, "maybe someday this book will come back to me as a gift, its pages filled." Credit for my writing also goes to my son Rahul for helping me develop material for the book.

The journey from seed-like, genetic potential to the fruition of my capacities, to whatever extent, has been a long one, across many frontiers. Along the way, there have been four phases or junctures of development. From these, I have begun to experience and understand what the inner life and the external world signify; also, the meanings of non-judgment, detachment, sub-ration, evolution, and transcendence have become clear. What, for me, is a practical way to a world of peace and prosperity? How can I enable and empower others around me to become active denizens of such a world?

This book is rooted in those exchanges and discusses those issues that are, I believe, of the utmost importance to us all. I have come to understand that both the inner world of the self and the external world of Nature are complex. The unfolding is like a pilgrimage. Will it be a journey on a well-known and ancient path or will it involve choices from among many holy paths? All paths, I will try to show, lead to the mountaintop. There might be, I warn, some stretches of passage that do not have a ready-made path. But perhaps that is one of the joys of pilgrimage.

Of Chasms and Bridges

I have also learned from my peak moments how bridges of peace—inner and external, personal and societal—can at times be built between groups that are at war and constantly violate each other. The social, political and economic space in which man lives today is extremely conflict-ridden; wars and now terrorism have claimed that space for themselves. The external situation mirrors an equally discordant internal one.

We see inside and around us existence that is fractured, life in pain. But how do we see what is wrong? An orthopedic surgeon x-rays a patient to see which of his bones have been broken and how. The traditional wisdom of Indian sages provides tools for seeing what has been broken in our inner selves and in our collective life, and indicates ways toward healing.

As the ancient sages described it, the three domains that make up our seemingly single, but total human self are: the somatic self of the human body, given at birth and taken away at death but perhaps extending beyond both borders; the psychic self, which is shaped or distorted as one grows up and in turn shapes or distorts us; and the spiritual self, at the metaphysical level.

Apart from these and interacting with them is Nature, from which the wealth of nations and individuals is produced. These four forces in mutual relationship produce our internal (as well as external) state, which can either be at peace or at war. Each of these selves can remain within its own bounds and achieve a degree of perfection, or can violate its own and other selves' boundaries. Such violation, sages tell us, is at the root of external and societal violence.

Bridges can be built in the inner world of our individual existence, as well as in the socio-political-economic world, to restore to a greater or lesser degree the present-day situation of war and terror to a state of peace and prosperity. To do so, the somatic and psychic selves must remain wholesome, healthy, and balanced, along with a healed and wholesome Nature.

Samskara: Reception, Cultivation, Education

I favor a practical approach, because I think that human suffering today could be lessened and the world could experience peace and prosperity, as Mahatma Gandhi in our own time and sages in ancient India wished, along with other great souls in many cultures. This could be achieved through firstly, placing the tools and power of *Samskara* at our disposal, and learning how to acquire, perfect and use them; and secondly, applying these tools judiciously and skillfully to the somatic and psychic selves and Nature as our fields of action, by organizing, cultivating, and educating each of these entities.

The wisdom of *Samskara* is not exclusive to any one culture. It is everywhere and in all traditions. Being pleasant and humble, attributes of *Samskara*, are traditions in many countries. *Samskara* in both Hindu and Buddhist traditions is associated with past karmas and desires from a previous life. The belief is that the good karma of past lives gives good *Samskara* in the next life and bad karma gives bad *Samskara*, somewhat analogous to Newton's third law of motion, which states that actions and reactions are equal and opposite. *Samskara* in Eastern traditions is not only the vestige of a person's karma, but also a dynamic force in a person's psychic self. However, I consider myself to be an "agnostic" and ignorant on matters of past lives.

I am interested only in this present life and only in good *Samskara*. Wherever the word *Samskara* is used in this book, it means good *Samskara*, to enable, with the right training and culturing of the prepsychic self, transcendence of the psychic and then the philosophic self, and ultimately the approach to the doorstep of the spiritual self.

If the inborn desire to know is taken as the first phase of my journey as a student of life, three more phases follow. The second has been the period of my education. By training, in India and the USA, I am an engineer. I worked as a researcher for a leading U.S. organization in aerospace technology. This is my acquired education and training—so-called "markings" from my teachers or early influences. In the Indian tradition, in the initiation ceremony, the guru puts markings on the body of the pupil. In most cases, they are specific lines drawn with sandalwood paste. During my education in the modern institutions of learning, research and work, it was not all sandalwood. There were times of considerable hardship.

The third phase of my *Samskaric* life began when I turned to the world of commerce. I was born into a family of successful businessmen and have been reasonably successful in my business in America. When the drive to acquire wealth culminated in success, I discovered that the same drive led me to a judicious distribution of my share of wealth. With that, I entered the fourth phase and, in a sense, the culmination of my *Samskaric* life. I found as much satisfaction in giving wealth to others as in acquiring wealth from society and Nature. This prompted me to support research and teaching in institutions like the University of California and Loyola Marymount University, both in Los Angeles, to propagate the ancient Indian ethical and spiritual values I learned in my youth. This early training must have marked me in some way, cultivated me in its own manner, and provided me with *Samskara* for a faraway future. My happy and fulfilling experience in giving away acquired wealth is somewhat similar to catching a fish and releasing it back to the water.

Ancient Heritage: Indian in Origin, Global in Scope

The great ancient heritage from India is a heritage for all mankind, not only for India. But a true, rich heritage is not easy to inherit. Typically, modernized Indians, who should lay first claim to these riches, have become disinherited and impoverished descendants of their wealthy forefathers. We shall try to see, in the chapters to follow, a general itinerary of this wealth of ancient India, the blocks (mostly set up by ourselves but also constructed forcibly by invaders and aggressors, both external and internal) in the pathways to that treasure, and the course corrections and occasional detours that have to be made by true seekers in order to circumnavigate obstacles to finally reach the destination—peace, prosperity, and joy for mankind.

We need to accept that the days of colonization, as it existed in the recent past, together with the sense of racial superiority are gone. We need to replace it by the sense of being connected based upon genetic discoveries.

Going back tens of thousands of years, we see our oldest great, great, great grandparents originating in Ethiopia. The African tribes of Homo sapiens migrated to India, Java and to Australia and central Asia, then moved to the west to Europe, and east to China, Alaska and finally to the Americas. Ever since then, we have been connected in some shape or form. And with today's technology of the Internet, cell phones and GPS systems, we are more connected than ever.

Humanity is now, more than ever before, transcending from individual consciousness, and moving toward a unified consciousness. This is all part of evolution within and evolution without. And now, we need to evolve more and faster within, that is, in the psychological domain. This is where the wisdom of scholars, saints and philosophers of the past and the present is indispensable to us.

Today, as the world struggles with war and terrorism, it is time to revisit that ancient heritage—"Where the entire world comes together in a single nest," says the Vedic sage. Such is the Indian directive and many pilgrims are turning to it.

So, let us begin our pilgrimage.

Chapter 2
The Somatic Self

The Three Domains of the Total Human Self

It is not easy to understand the totality of the human self. The human body manifests traces of evolution from the simplest forms of life to the most complex. Man finds himself in Nature and finds Nature in himself; in fact, man is a veritable museum of Nature. Nature expresses itself in man and his multi-domain self and brings meaning to God's creation. While modern Western scientific studies of body and mind provide us with many tools to understand man's make-up, Western scientists show a conspicuous lack of curiosity about Eastern wisdom. In the manner of such inquirers as the Indian psychologist Nirmal Kumar and the eminent scientist Dr. D. S. Kothari, it is advisable to look into the many ways of understanding the human self, without limiting inquiry to any one tradition of knowledge.

The total human self includes the three domains of somatic, psychic and spiritual. The relationship of these different domains with Nature produces wealth as well as health, if that relationship is based on wisdom and not merely on reason. The absence or lack of wisdom can produce misery and ill-health. How can we best keep the somatic, psychic, and spiritual domains autonomous and in harmony with Nature in a creative, productive, peaceful way?

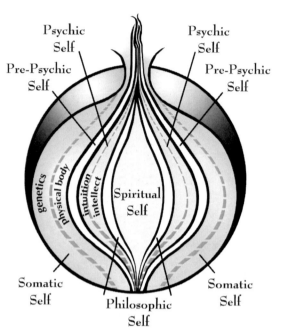

Figure 2-1 The Layers and Sub-Layers of the Total Human Self

Let us look closely at the dimensions of the human self and its derivatives. If we observe our own self, we will see that there are many layers to it, somewhat like the layers of an onion bulb, each separate and independent with a flexible boundary. It is as though Nature used one material to form one part of man, and then took up an entirely different material to begin another part; and so on. There is the body, tangible and visible; and the mind or psyche, which motivates us. Then, as the saints and ancient masters would remind us, there is the spirit or soul.

The somatic self has two aspects: the body and the DNA. It functions automatically, with pulsing nerves and reflexes, a rhythmic heart, and self- regulating temperature control and blood pressure. The somatic self is neither subordinate nor superior to the other two selves; it is independent and autonomous, just as they are. The somatic self contains an element of the pre-psychic self. The somatic self is independent of, yet connected to, the psychic self. It is the domain of primal urges and energies.

The psychic self also has two aspects: the intellect and intuition. The intellectual mind is the seat of reason and logic. The intuitive mind is the seat of love and other emotions, like compassion and forgiveness.

The spiritual self is the domain of the soul. Ancient Indian sages who composed the *Vedas* and Vedanta have depicted it. The word "Veda" means "to know," and the word "Vedanta" indicates "the end of or culmination of knowledge." The philosopher points beyond the finite to the infinite, from the knowable to something beyond human knowledge and out of the domain of Nature, meaning non-local, and beyond human comprehension.

As a first step toward integration, it is necessary for us to accept, non-judgmentally, our somatic self as an autonomous and independent entity. Once this is accepted, it becomes possible to refine and cultivate the animal power of the somatic self, and to control the wild ruler and its needs and energies. Indian civilization kept the basic impulses and desires thus educated through an understanding of the autonomy of the three selves. Social customs, religious rites, and legal systems all contributed to this. Indian tradition held that the refinement and cultivation of bodily desires, the somatic impulses, could be achieved through the science of *Samskara*.

The Qualities of the Somatic Self

The ancient sages of India would say in essence that life comes out of "death," that is, chaos, and the body of the baby in the mother's womb comes to life gradually. The evolutionary process takes over. Initially chaotic, the order and complexity of the organism keep increasing. These processes are natural and the best of Nature; intelligence is not needed to keep the heart beating. The inside of the body functions "divinely," similar to the rising sun and the moon. The baby out of the womb learns to walk and talk by instinct more than anything else. There is hardly any place for intellect.

The ancient sages of India connected genetics with the actions of the past life; one gets a good genetic make-up if the karma of the past life is good. In this book, genetics is considered as the initial condition of order attached to chance more than karma. Ancients, however, believed that God's creation is due to God's playfulness, implying that life is God's game and chance is attached to all games.

The somatic self is the primal base of our total self. It includes physical vigor that at times gets involved in mischievous activities. The world of the somatic self is like the movement of fish in deep waters, apparently showing no pattern, a movement without rules, without meaning, in constant flux. A world that is ever-changing, kaleidoscopic, and anarchic, cannot provide stability for knowledge. The existential depth of our somatic self cannot be approached with the classical obsession with "being," as it is a world of ceaseless "becoming." "Being" is a separate non-participating state, as when a scientist observes or measures parameters like temperature without disturbing the observed process. While "becoming" is when a participant experiences a process, for example, dancers on a stage performing a dance.

I am reminded of a strong personality, the powerful prime minister of India, Indira Gandhi. She once said, "Poverty is the greatest polluter." She was expressing the ageless wisdom of India, and what she said reminded me of an ancient Tamil proverb, "All ten virtues will disappear in the face of hunger." If one looks at both these quotes, one sees that without taking care of the somatic self, without caring for basic human needs first, nothing lasting can be achieved in any other domain of the human personality. The somatic self, disregarded and disgraced, rejects psychological and spiritual advancement, and in such circumstances war and violence become the principal amoral activities of an imbalanced society. Like a shark that is hungry, the somatic self will kill and eat, caring little for anything else; it does not discriminate in selecting its victims. However, through right education and training (but not through externally imposed conditioning and straight-jacketing by fanaticism), this "human shark" can be transformed into a dynamo of positive energy for creative activities in society.

The impulses and energies of the body cannot be governed through the willful expression of the psychic self. This causes further problems and distortions, defiance and explosions, as the Western world has learned through bitter experience. Man without training cannot overpower and suppress physical hunger and bodily urges; if suppressed, they may take sinister forms. An effective way of dealing with the impulses, needs and energies of the body is to treat the somatic self with due respect, as a separate autonomous domain of human personality. In ancient India, skillful and insightful teachers trained their young students for years until the process of imparting *Samskara* to the somatic self was completed. This was the core course, compulsory for all students.

The training of the intellect was subsequent to it. A tendency of modern man is to mix the somatic and psychic selves and to submit the former to the dictates of the latter. The result is that we have made the body and the mind slaves to reason and logic, which were originally tools of the total self. But now they have become masters, dictating their own terms and conditions to body and mind. Indian philosophical systems, such as Jainism and Buddhism, caution against this. The intellect is indeed one of the derivatives in Nature, but Nature does not play slave to intellect. Rhythmic patterns in Nature have achieved a perfection of their own, quite independent of intellect. The waves of the ocean, the stars and the sun in the sky, the beating of the heart in human and other living beings—how perfect are their rhythms, and how independent of intellectual control or interference. Man is soul, but man is Nature too. For peace and inner harmony, the activities of one should not interfere with the activities of the other.

We can distinguish three types of "thinking"—somatic, psychic and spiritual. If these are mixed to make a soup, they could result in mental disorders and produce fanatics and maniacs. An intelligent racist could easily put forward a logical and convincing argument in favor of racism. Man has today become more brutal and violent in spite of all advances in logic and reason, or perhaps because of that. All three types of thinking are of equal importance. Each of them should be autonomous and coexist, and none should overpower the others. Our civilization is doomed if it permits this to happen.

In the ancient Indian system of education, which included the discipline of yoga, the somatic self was trained and made "*Samskaric.*" Ancient teachers prompted people to ask questions about the somatic self. How is it ruled or governed? The ruler of the somatic self lies in the human genitalia or reproductive organs. This ruler is not only a wild pleasure-seeker but also a ruthless dictator with an excess of animal energy that needs to be tamed and trained.

Indian civilization has always insisted on finding and perfecting methods to bring basic impulses and desires under self-control. For this it has employed laws, religious and social customs, and other ways to strengthen *Samskara*. Indian tradition has held that refining and cultivating somatic energy and desires should be done through the rites of *Samskara*, which deal with the somatic self in its own terms, without imposing strictures and commands from either the psychic or spiritual realms. That keeps the somatic self autonomous and separate from the psychic self. The implications of such autonomy and separation at the macro-level, for socio-economic activities in interaction with Nature, are discussed in Chapter 4.

In ancient India, the process of imparting *Samskara* began through scriptures and customs required of parents and families to engage in three types of rituals. The first took place at the very inception of life in the womb of a young woman as a mother; the second when the life in the womb had taken up a certain identity; the third, the ceremony of name-giving, soon after the birth of a child. This links the somatic self, which for life at its very beginning is the pre-dominant aspect of existence, to parents, family, and the immediate community through love.

Ancient Indian sages knew with great clarity the difference between suppression and cultivation on the one hand, and between cultivation and wild growth on the other. Indian tradition held that the refinement and cultivation of somatic impulses and bodily desires through *Samskara* would help man dispense with external, intellectual checks imposed on his primal and energetic somatic self. Such impositions lead only to distortion and violence. Man cannot overpower or fully suppress the hungers and impulses of the body. Jihadist terrorism from one tradition and psychotic shoot-outs in high schools in another tradition are examples of such sinister distortions of personality.

One way to see how the somatic self has been made *Samskaric* is to check how it responds to external stimuli: a response could be an over-reaction, as occurs in a coiled spring or in the stretched wire of a musical instrument; or it could be sluggish, as occurs in a massive object. Both are inappropriate. It could be said that Western civilization trains the somatic self to respond in the mode of over-reaction. A Western person sometimes jumps into action, at individual and collective levels. At the social level, crime rates and individual and family violence in Western societies are cause for alarm. On the other hand, Eastern societies, states and individuals are open to charges of sluggish, lethargic responses to stimuli. Problems do not get solved, assaults and invasions are not anticipated and countered, and wealth and freedom are oftentimes lost. A somatic self that has received *Samskara* would not err either way, and would aid individuals, society, and the state.

There is no end to the desires and greed of the body. Carl Jung derived the word "libido" from the Sanskrit word *lobhayati*, meaning "greed-causing." There is still much that needs to be discovered about the human body, and much that had once been discovered but forgotten needs to be recollected and remembered. There are today many inhibitions that place the body under stress. What, then, is true freedom of the somatic self? True physical freedom is born out of a rigorous cultural exercise that transfers impulses, instincts and reflexes into a relaxed body. A glimpse of physical freedom is seen in the ancient Indian sculptures of Shiva and Vishnu, Buddha and Mahavira; their bodies are perfectly relaxed and at ease.

The Cultivation of the Pre-Psychic Self and Samskara Training

The next stage is of developing the pre-psychic sub-layer within the somatic domain. The pre-psychic self is the bridge between the somatic self, where there is very little light, and the brighter psychic self. *Samskaric* principles guide the training and culturing of physical impulses and reflexes, including the integration and development of harmony of pairs of opposites.

Both violence and nonviolence occur first at the level of the body. Here the concept and practice of violence and nonviolence are tested most realistically; they are not only spiritual concepts, as projected by Gandhi and King during their freedom struggles. Claims have been made that there is a connection of different human attributes, like faith and (non)violence, hardwired into our genes. The ancient sages of India also associated genes with human attributes. However, there is ample evidence that *Samskaric* training helps to develop the best of human attributes, including lasting peace.

The ancient builders of Indian culture stated that beyond the realm of reason there is the realm of darkness, where demons capture intellect (reasoning and speech), and even gods cannot help. In essence Buddha said the same: the intellect could take over the mind and turn us into devils. Positive life-fulfilling spontaneity is a prerequisite for a healthy psychic self. The pre-psychic sub-layer, though a part of the somatic self, connects to the psychic self. Such a cultivation of the pre-psychic self can be achieved only through understanding the body's own language.

The nerves that spread out in the brain, the heart, and every part of the human body form a separate world, a dark world, which reason cannot illuminate. This dark world of the somatic self is neither moral nor immoral, and it cannot be dealt with or judged by the ethics of psychology or spirituality. We cannot learn about ourselves, employing all the tools at our disposal, by dividing ourselves into parts; knowledge of the whole is different from knowledge of the parts.

The human impulses of sympathy, compassion and non-violence are intuitive and spontaneous; they are the very essence of being human. Even in scientific discovery, it is not enough to employ the intellect, however brilliant. Persistence, endurance, resilience, and intuition—all are required. They form the attributes of a *Samskaric* personality, acquired through hard training, strong will, and discipline, always positive thinking, optimistic, and looking for the good in the worst of us.

How is this process initiated and into what does it culminate? It is done through the integration of opposites, to be achieved in all areas of bodily experience. That is why the ancient Indian masters of yoga and other pathways maintained that enlightenment was not possible without the human body. The body experience does not contradict the spiritual experience, according to the Indian sages. Nature exposes its transcendental truths by means of physical, bodily sensations. *Samskara* is the cause of the enduring athlete, of fine musicians, and the acrobats of Cirque du Soleil, giving pleasure to the audience.

Reality and being are like a tree. The roots, trunk, branches, leaves, flowers and seeds look like a multiplicity. There are levels of being, neither disconnected nor discontinuous, although under the influence of divisional analytical science, we might take them to be so. But the ancient sages and the *Gita*, the bible of the East, speak of a tree that has its roots upward and its branches growing downward, a tree that neither deteriorates nor changes. So we cannot talk of one level being better or superior to the other. Each level of being is complete in itself. Each level has its own light; the light of one level is darkness for another. Intermixing is never helpful. What is required is to transcend as a forward and unidirectional process.

Feminine and masculine aspects are present in every human being. Ancient Indian art created the image of Lord Shiva with the half-body of man and the other half of woman. Women need to be treated as equal, neither as inferior as in some fundamentalist societies, nor as superior as in some so-called advanced societies.

Modern Western psychology refers to the unconscious in the human psyche, extensively documented by Sigmund Freud. The unconscious is seen by some to be diabolic. This, I suspect, happens when our view is restricted or filtered through merely the psychic aspect of the human self. The somatic self, consisting of the human body and genetics, linking it to an extended scheme of time, has its own hungers, impulses, thought-like urges, which have to be satisfied, trained and cultured. Deeper than the pre-psychic domain but within the somatic self, are shades of darkness that become darker as one goes deeper.

In different ways, one can learn to train the pre-psychic self. Ancient sages employed examples and stories to teach their students. I came across a modern story about a mother who taught her daughter, not by pampering her, but through love that knew how to be tender and tough at the same time. It is the story of a carrot, an egg, and a cup of coffee.

The young woman told her mother how difficult things were for her. The mother took the daughter to the kitchen, where she boiled three pots of water. She then asked her daughter to put a carrot in one pot, an egg in another, and some coffee grains in the third.

The girl did as she was asked, puzzled and amused. After 20 minutes, the mother asked her daughter to take out the carrot and the egg and put them in two bowls, and to pour the liquid from the third pot into a mug. After letting each cool, the mother asked her daughter to see how the carrot felt to her touch. "Soft," said the girl. "And the egg? Break the shell and look inside." "Hard," said the daughter. The mother asked her daughter to sip the liquid in the mug. "It is coffee, of course," the daughter exclaimed, "but what does all this mean and how does it make things less difficult for me?" "It does not change your circumstances," said the mother, "but it prompts you to see that there are at least three ways in which you can respond to your situation."

"My situation is like this boiling water!" said the daughter, beginning to understand.

"Yes, darling," the mother said, "the boiling water has made the once-hard carrot soft. That is the first option. The second option is suggested by the egg," continued the mother. "The boiling water made it hard inside."

"That is my option," cried the daughter.

"But first sip some coffee," said the mother with a smile.

"What have the coffee beans done to the water?" The daughter stared at the mug and then at the mother, who said, "Yes, now you get it. The coffee beans have changed the boiling water to coffee." The young girl knew then that, just like the hardy coffee beans, she could change her trying and difficult circumstances to her own color and flavor.

In the ancient Indian scriptures, deep insights are found about each of the three domains of the total human self. The *Vedas* generally speak of the somatic domain, while the *Upanishads* speak of the spiritual, and the *Puranas* of the psychological. Indian sages perceive the mind as a stage on which consciousness acts, but they also make it clear that the somatic self is not to be equated with the unconscious. Again, consciousness is not limited to the state of staying awake; sleep is not inferior to the state of being awake. Wakefulness and sleep are two different states of our being, neither inferior to the other. Both states are necessary; we interact with nature external to us when we are awake. We come closest to our spiritual being (Atman) when we are in the state of deep sleep when body and mind are not active; Atman is the cause of us being rested and refreshed when we wake up from deep sleep.

Yet another state of being is that which is neither awake nor asleep, neither conscious nor unconscious, neither rational nor irrational. The state of being is in synchrony with Nature and regulates such rhythmic phenomena as the beating of the heart; the cycle of birth, decay and death; the movements of the planets. It is the power that ancient Indians called *Samskara,* the disciplined and essentially human driving-force of the somatic self. Samskara is the cause of optimism and positive thinking.

Ancient Indian sages recognized the importance and autonomy of both consciousness and the somatic self. Both are tied to Nature. If consciousness looks upon itself as the ultimate state of being, supreme and absolute, it creates problems, socially as well as psychologically. Indian sages looked at consciousness as an inner space, not as an absolute. It was a part of Nature, seen by Indian scriptures to have three qualities, which are simultaneously at play in the human body too: consciousness, *Samskaras* (human impulses in sync with Nature), and pain with decay and suffering. Indian sages have presented the system and the practice of yoga to strike a balance between the three qualities and their powers. When the three are in perfect balance and harmony, no longer self-centered, the body enters into a state of meditation. Then the body becomes part of the universe and is in harmony with all that is in Nature—the trees, mountains, streams, and the rest. Salvation lies in getting beyond the boundaries between the body and the universe.

Ancient Indians believed in striving for the best with diligence, signifying somatic spontaneities for the earthly objectives of possessions and sex. However, these objectives were to be pursued within the bounds of cultural and moral duty, signifying the limits set up by natural laws. The three dimensions of the human personality—the somatic, psychic, and spiritual—have their own inlaid principles. When man transits from one to the other, following these principles from one dimension to the next, he discovers an amazing alignment leading to liberation, *Moksha, Nirvana*, and relief from bondage. If man has failed to create a beautiful and pleasant world, one of the causes is his ignorance of his somatic self. In the somatic depth of each male, there is his feminine half. In being unjust to womankind, every man becomes unjust to the feminine half of his own somatic self, disturbing the somatic balance within.

Samskara and Ruta

In this context, the concept of *Ruta*, central in Indian tradition, needs to be introduced. *Ruta* is Universal and Eternal Truth or Ultimate Reality or *Brahman* in its dynamic, temporal, material form. *Ruta* is Nature in its best mood, benevolent, loving, and truthful. It is the first evolute, the first incarnate of Nature.

[*Samskara* and *Ruta* are intimately related. *Samskara* is the energy and the feminine side of *Ruta*, which is operational through *Samskara*. When the somatic self is cultivated and develops *Samskara*, *Ruta* becomes accessible. *Ruta* is the spirit within the grain, the fragrance of the rose, and the joy in music. In short, *Ruta* is the essence of Nature. God created *Ruta*, the first evolute of Nature-a very first conceivable form of being, its second part being the finest form of intellect, and the source being the somatic self. *Ruta* is the force that creates rhythmic existence out of anarchic disorder, harmony out of cacophony.

It has been noted by Vedic scholars that in the *Rig Veda* there is a remarkable insight on the notion of *Ruta* or cosmic order, the inflexible, unchangeable, absolute law of universal order and harmony whereby all disorders and chaos are restored to equilibrium. *Ruta* is, in essence, the ordering principle of Nature that gives to everything, from the vast galaxies down to the nucleus of an atom, its nature and course.

In the Vedic vision, this law of cosmic order manifests at three levels:

• On the cosmic mega-level, *Ruta* governs the course of Nature, the movements of stars and planets, the cycle of seasons, and so on.

• On the socio-ethical, macro-level, *Ruta* imparts justice, keeps the social and ethical order moving smoothly; and

• On the subtlest micro-level, *Ruta* is the cause to receive spontaneous revelations, and insights through meditation. At this subtlest level, Ruta also governs the laws of quantam mechanics and the science of sub-atomic particles.

It is the responsibility of *Ruta* to keep and maintain balance and harmony within and between each level. *Ruta* also denotes the order of moral law. As the great Indian thinker and former president of India, Dr. S. Radhakrishnan has explained, "*Ruta* originally meant the established route of the world, of the sun, moon and stars, morning and evening, day and night. Gradually it becomes the path of morality to be followed by man and the law of righteousness observed even by gods."

In the hymns of the *Rig Veda*, *Ruta* signifies the idea of a fundamental lawfulness of nature, the law being construed both as the law of truth and as a moral law that none, not even the gods, could transgress. This conception of *Ruta* emerges as the more familiar law of karma, of moral causation that becomes more important than the idea of God. *Ruta* is hidden in the human body, mind, and in Nature. It is inscribed in the genetic codes of all living beings. It is *Ruta* that creates and constitutes our health, is psychological truth, a healthy mind.

Tremendous psychological disorders could be caused through even small manipulations and imbalances in the somatic powers. Every human person has his or her unique combination of somatic powers given by Nature. To keep them in balance, and to keep the pre-psychic self at peace, is a better way to a beautiful and pleasant future.

We all long to live in a world at peace. We all wish, for ourselves and others, health, wealth and wisdom. But before achieving this, we must travel from anarchy to order, from conflict and disorder to a rhythmic existence within ourselves and in tune with Nature. There are no shortcuts to a sane, peaceful, prosperous and productive society or individual, and no pathway to such a society or individual can ever neglect the somatic self, which holds the keys to many treasures and abundant energy.

Chapter 3

The Psychic Self

The Psychological Domain: Its Limitations and Strengths

The process of transcendence from the somatic to the psychic self can be stated simply. First, there needs to be non-judgment of all other levels, and each self should be autonomous within its own domain. Autonomy is the prerequisite to detachment, detachment to sub-ration, and sub-ration to transcendence.

The psychological or psychic domain of the human self at both individual and collective levels is, perhaps, in need of some basic reorientation in today's strife-torn world. As the first step, it is necessary to understand what the psychic self is and how it functions or malfunctions. A fundamental misconception about the psychological self, its relation to the somatic self on the one hand and the spiritual self on the other, has led to much current mischief and conflict. The ancient Indian understanding of the human psyche has, in my view, much to offer here and might well provide the key to the solution of such problems as global terrorism and historical conflicts leading to series of wars and other devastations.

While the psychological domain of the human personality is independent and autonomous, we see today a great deal of mixing of the psychic and somatic selves, the former intruding into the latter and imposing its own solutions, which prove to be worse than the problems they try to solve. Imposed solutions from the third domain, the spiritual self, also add to complications and distortions.

Ancient Indian psychology presents a strikingly different understanding of the human psychic self, an excellent account of which has been provided by the eminent thinker, Nirmal Kumar. Vedic mythology, which is understood as a concealed treatise on human psychology, says that when the psychic self is born out of the somatic self, it coils around the somatic mother through fear of separation from it. When the psyche overcomes this fear, it experiences the reality of the two domains. The psychic self can realize psychological monism, which enables it to be free of the suffering of separation from the somatic.

Thus separated, the psychological self, transcends and moves toward an empty beyond to realize its destiny, but without guidance from the somatic self. This is because the two domains function independently of each other and a separation must be maintained to avoid the corruption of both.

What then is the task before the psychic self, according to ancient Indian psychology? The highest achievement of the psychological self is in spontaneous love, as illustrated in Indian mythology through the figures of Radha and Krishna. They are able to purge their psychic selves of all bondage through their love for each other. Their total personalities find fullest realization in their mutual unconditional love and in the full, pure joy of their psyches, which struggled to overcome the primal fear of separation mentioned above. There are no somatic desires associated with love including that of sex.

Though born out of the physical energies of the somatic self, the psychic self has its own aspirations. It has glimpses of a heavenly world never seen on earth; it wants to be weightless, soar to any height unchecked, disregarding material things including gold, since it fears matter. Moving against gravity is the process of sub-ration and transcendence.

The strength of the psychic self is in its vision and detachment from worldly things. Its vision is noble though unrealistic, and when challenged, it finds difficulty in countering the challenge; it is of the beautiful and good, but is powerless in a material world. It is like an angel flapping its wings aimlessly, with all those clever materialists aiming to shoot it down like a game bird.

Yet the psychological self is universally present in each one of us and cannot be brushed aside or wished away. Religious fanatics have taken advantage of its shattered dreams of beauty and truth by building a religiously sanctioned heaven and asking the masses to submit to their preaching. The time has come to liberate the psychological self from religious and materialist zealots.

The psychic and somatic selves are two different realities, neither less than the other nor to be judged by the standards of the other. They are differently equipped, mutually exclusive, like two different species of Nature—a pigeon cannot be an eagle and an eagle cannot be a pigeon.

Mahavira and Buddha did not speak of a permanent and spiritual soul. They talked of the psychological self as an ever-changing, ever-evolving reality within us, and they talked of its liberation, enabling man to transcend to a higher level. The psychic self has a vision of Absolute that is the vision of permanence; the permanent is the ideal, the one the psychic self strives for.

Without a liberated psychological self, none can enter the domain of the spiritual. It is the stepping stone on the path to Realization, and thus is mother of the spiritual self.

Vedic sages have described several souls within us. The psychological self is the integrating or connecting force, a string that keeps connected all that man contains—procreation, self-importance, imagination, virtue, intuition, science and religion, spiritual aspiration, love and intellect. If the string is broken, the gems fall apart, inviting looters within and without. These constituents of the psychic self can only transcend by keeping their right proportions. Man needs to be careful that any one of these components does not enslave his psychic self.

As an independent entity, the psychic self is the link and bridge between the worldly somatic self and the metaphysical spiritual self.

The spiritual self is universal and disinterested in individual egos. The somatic self, on the other hand, is incapable of comprehending larger issues. When India was invaded from outside, the conquerors' theories invaded the psychological self of ancient Indians and inflicted atrocities on it. The theories of the invaders came from their own spiritual development, a kind of imposed spiritual Nazism. Under its authority, the somatic and psychological selves of the Indians became slaves of the invaders' spiritual self.

Indians have always had a passion for synthesis. However, on the pretense of synthesis, they accepted alien ideas to mix with their own, losing their autonomy, hoping to establish brotherhood and love for the invaders. Indians have gone to any lengths to accommodate the opposite, by regression, to avoid strife and violence. Ancient Vedic Indians knew that all three dimensions of the total human self—somatic, psychic, and spiritual—were equal to each other. All pathways, insists Indian tradition, are equally correct and useful in reaching Reality.

Spiritualism in Indian tradition has never been despotic; the somatic and psychological selves have never been subjected to the dictates of the spiritual domain in any Indian tradition, be it Vedic, Buddhist or Jain. Monks and sages were free to paint, carve and sing of the somatic and psychological selves. Union of the two was depicted in paintings and sculptures in the caves of Ajanta and Ellora and countless other magnificent places. The poetry and plays of Valmiki and Vyasa, Kalidasa and Bhasa, depicted the somatic and psychological selves as well as the spiritual self, without pontific, eulogistic interference or disapproval.

Man has suffered as much under spiritual Nazism as under material Nazism. The forces that inflicted spiritual atrocities have also inflicted material extortions on India. Consider the apt words of South African leader, Desmond Tutu, "They came and gave us the Bible and took from us our land in return."

The Avoidance of Regression and Mixing; The Maintenance of Autonomy

The greatest error of modern psychology, convincingly argued by Nirmal Kumar, has been to mix the somatic and the psychological. Their union cannot create brotherhood and love; instead it creates hatred and violence. It is only through *Samskara* that the somatic self of man has its separate identity away from the animal kingdom. The ideal of the spiritual self is an unchanging, perennial truth, unlike the partial reality of the somatic self. The truth of the spiritual domain impedes the psychological self, because it arrests its movement and flux and stifles its growth. Bilateral communication and constant dialogue are the major constituents of the psychic self. Unidirectional communication by a teacher or a parent becomes indoctrination. Recall Nagarjuna's statement, almost two millennia back in India: "Buddha was a magnificent reality empirically, and magnificent illusion spiritually," which distinguishes distinctly between the psychological and spiritual selves.

An example of the perversion resulting from mixing the psychological and somatic dimensions can be found in our decision-making process at election times every four or five years in democratic nations. Though it is such an important decision, we tend to confuse aspects of the somatic selves of the candidates for aspects of their psychological selves, like modes of speech and communication. An individual with good looks, charm, and commanding body language often has a better chance of getting elected, regardless of the level of his wisdom.

The Dalai Lama is much less likely to succeed obtaining autonomy for Tibetans from Chinese rulers since the former communicates in a psychic domain that cannot be comprehended by the Chinese rulers functioning in mixed domains for their advantage.

Many scholars would agree that the most disastrous religious movement of late has been the jihadist used by fundamentalist Muslim sects like Hamas and the Taliban to advocate violence. These jihadist sects have certain qualities in common. For one, they insist on simple and total obedience from their followers based on an emotionally clouded perception of "God's Will." In a study of the economics of religious extremism, Professor Eli Berman of the University of California at San Diego has shown how the centers of jihadist religious sects have at their center strong economic motives.

From an observer's point of view, it can be seen clearly that one of the problems of the jihadists' philosophy and extremism lies in its mixing of the psychological or devotional self with the somatic self. One of the key problems of certain religions throughout their histories is that they do not allow the three dimensions of the total human self to exist side by side. In fact, the denial of separateness, autonomy, and equality to the somatic, psychological, and spiritual selves can and does lead to severe mental illness and a distorted and sick personality.

On the face of it, jihadist culture and its violent and devastating activities, religious or otherwise, do not go well with economics. Jihadist leaders ask their devotees to give up all worldly pleasures and pursuits. This is disastrous for the economy of any nation governed by such leaders, since consumption is essential in an economic system.

Men and women work to acquire the ability to consume more, not less. This is famously known as Economics 101. However, in many ascetic religious traditions, devotees forgo material pleasures to reap rewards in an afterlife. Such self-control is not necessarily a bad thing; on the contrary, most consider it to be good. However, it is our purpose here to distinguish good ascetic traditions that contribute to the health of the psychological self rather than the exploitative, destructive practices of jihadist sects. Two instances of good, contributive ascetic movements will clarify this issue.

Ianna Cone, a professor at George Mason University, undertook, some years back, a landmark economic study of the Amish community in Pennsylvania as well as the Mormon community in Utah. She discovered that the economic benefits and profits from a strict religious life are often greater than the cost. These benefits and profits may come in the form of "public good." This includes good education, food for the needy, law and order, and a lower crime rate. Professor Cone found that the stricter the inner discipline of a religious group, the more "public good" it generated.

The example of the Hare Krishna Community is also before us. Men and women of this community get up early in the morning at four or five o'clock and work hard all day long. Some members run small-scale industries, like candle-making, and manage to live on a small stipend in housing provided by the community. This might look like voluntary imprisonment, but the members say that they are living a happy life now and looking forward to a promising afterlife.

Many Christian monastic traditions, like the Benedictines, have long functioned on similar principles of self-discipline, prayer, asceticism, living on a meager income, and community living, with their basic needs provided for by the order. In India, there have been many such great and small traditions of self-disciplined, austere, hardworking, service-oriented, religious groups and movements.

An example is that of a remarkable man, Pandurang Athavale. Through a well-organized, voluntary movement called "Self-Trained Family," he practically educated millions of people in the western state of Gujarat, and motivated them to undertake a life of hard, voluntary work toward a society free from vices and active in its faith in God and good deeds. He and his large group of volunteers went from village to village, home to home, bringing about dramatic changes in community life. Husbands who were alcoholic, wasted their earnings, and beat up their wives and children gradually became caring fathers, husbands, and self-disciplined members of their communities. As these examples show, asceticism can be good for society and for the "common good," even if it poses a challenge to marketplace benefits and commerce in goods and services.

The question today is how to distinguish between destructive and authoritarian religious sects on the one hand, and religious movements that contribute to the public good and well-being. It has to be conceded that even the most destructive of sectarian movements, like the Taliban and Hamas, must be contributing to the economic and other benefits of their followers and others, and that there has to be an economic logic underneath the self-negation and control in the lives of their followers.

Instead of focusing on trade in drugs and extortions, kidnapping and ransom, and so on, that fuel terrorism's economics, I would focus on the problem of poverty in these societies that breeds fodder for terrorism, and produces young men and women who get killed while killing others. Poverty is the breeding ground for religious extremism and terrorism, whether in Pakistan, Afghanistan, or elsewhere. Our real question should be: How do we turn jihadists into productive members of a thriving economy?

The solution seems to be that governments and NGOs need to compete with fundamentalist jihadists to supply superior "public good" to the people. Had the former government of Afghanistan provided better public services and goods to its people, the influence of the Taliban would have become insignificant, in spite of their fundamentalist sectarian appeal. If better institutions are provided to poorer parts of the world, communities living in them will not see terrorism as an option.

The main task before us then is this: How does one keep the three domains of the total human self separate, ensuring that the demands and commands of one do not constrain and distort any of the others? But, simultaneously, it has to be seen how the progressive activities within one domain could become conducive to progression in another domain.

Of Two Birds and Two Dogs

How does one deal with the strengths and weaknesses, the productive and destructive forces of the psychological self? As stated earlier, Man is Nature's living museum. Not only that, but within him reside attributes of every creature, good and bad, both the successes and failures of Nature. These form the complexity of the human mind where man is a multidimensional adventure of Nature. Ancient Indian sages have made great efforts over centuries to understand this complexity, and the results of their search have dazzled and provided much light to mankind.

Professor Houston Smith of the University of California in Berkeley has observed that three great civilizations of the world have made three significant contributions to mankind. Western civilization provided the knowledge of Nature; Chinese civilization brought about the development of sociology; and Indian civilization produced a profound awareness and understanding of psychology through its scriptures.

Today, as the world reels under the blows of wars and engulfing terrorism, the Indian genius of understanding the human psyche could provide a way out of the world of intolerance and violence and a path toward a world of understanding, peace and prosperity. "Lead me from darkness to light" was the prayer of ancient India. As we watch our present world of aggression, torture and terror, it is time, once again, to revisit man's ancient heritage. It is urgent that mankind understand the formation, function, and possible evolution of the human psyche.

I am reminded of the symbolic imagery in a story from the *Gita*. "Two friendly companion birds together reside on one tree. One of them is eating the tree's fruits while the other does not eat but simply watches his friend." The finite soul, *Atman in nature*, and the infinite soul, *Brahman beyond nature*, are being compared with these two birds. Each retains its own separate entity while sharing the tree. One bird enjoys the fruits of the tree, the offerings of Nature. The other retains its independence, autonomy, and supremacy yet relates to the bird who, in turn, relates to Nature. The existence of the bird in Nature is relative, while the observer bird is really not in Nature but in the realm of the Absolute. The pair of birds represent a pair of opposites—an observer and a participant. However, they complement and are in harmony with each other and Nature. There is an important message here. Brahman's creation, nature, always creates pairs of opposite within our selves and in nature. Every pair should be in balance and each element should complement the other bringing harmony and prosperity.

The interaction between the somatic, psychic, and spiritual selves, as well as between each of these selves and Nature, takes place ceaselessly in a process synonymous with life. This interaction, if not cultivated or educated by *Samskara*, quickly produces conflicts, wars and terrorism.

It is ironic that most of the troubled spots in our world were in the past well-known places of beauty and peace, to which visitors from far-off lands traveled. The Middle East, the holiest place for three major religions of mankind, is now a zone of jihadic wars and mindless terror. Kashmir in India, once a center of learning, meditation and peace, is still a target for terrorism.

What goes wrong in these places? What is the deep structure of these and others round the globe? Eastern thought has taught us for thousands of years to coexist with two opposite views. It is a teaching that fundamentalist religions and some Western thinkers have unfortunately rejected, giving rise to jihadist mentalities and to terrorism. On the other hand, Eastern wisdom teaches us that there is something of good and something of evil in every man and every society, forming a pair of opposites. Evil here is ignorance and the raw material of the good. One has to learn the art of avoiding the dark side and thriving on the illuminated side of the mind. If this and other sound principles of ancient Indian psychology are accepted, in place of the conflict-oriented and guilt- ridden psychology proposed by modern psychologists, the zones of war and terrorism could be turned into places of peace and prosperity without paying a high human and economic cost.

There is a story of an Indian elder, not from ancient India but from pre-modern America. Wisdom has been distributed by God all around the globe. This American Indian chief was once asked how many dogs he had in his tent and what kind of dogs they were. The old chief replied that he had two dogs, one good, one bad. What do you do to these two dogs, he was asked, keep the bad one chained or caged and beaten and the good one free and pampered? "No," replied the wise old man, "I keep the good dog well-fed and give the other dog a little less, but still keep him well and alive in my own tent. I also spend more time to train him. I do need the services of both at any future moment for my travels or protection." He encouraged and emphasized the good within more than the bad.

The two birds of the *Gita* teach us something sublime. The two dogs of the Indian chief teach us something practical. The sublime and the practical are two sides of the same coin and the two Indians, one from the East, the other from the West, are not a world apart. Each is separate, but the two are relative too—in more than one sense of the word. Every one of us is no farther than a 33rd cousin of any other human being. This is on the basis that within 33 generations, multiplying two 33 times we would encompass the whole human population of less than eight billion. With clarity, it is possible and profitable to turn to our ancient past in order to meet our immediate future.

To turn calamities into opportunities is a challenge that our immediate future has thrown up to us, and which the psychology of the ancient sages empowers us to take on.

Life has to be looked at in its totality, even when at first glance it might show contradictions and fractures. Some violence-prone, fundamentalist cultures and religions might insist on accepting only what is taken by them to be the good and illuminated parts of life, and banish and hate what is taken to be the dark side, said to belong to Satan or the Devil. This promotion and rejection soon gives rise to conflicts.

Features of Balance and Harmony: Equality, Autonomy, Evolution, Non-Judgment and Detachment

As we have seen, the total human self has three domains: somatic, psychic and spiritual. The problems of one realm can never be solved if the solution is looked for in another realm. The wisdom of the ancient Indian sages tells us not to mix up these selves, not to look for solutions to the problems of one realm by imposing solutions that are alien to it. Problems of the somatic self cannot be solved by solutions of the psychic level. The challenges of the psychic self have to be met through solutions from the psychic self.

At an individual level, if the psychic self needs to be cured of excessive carnal desires, the solution can hardly be found by putting women behind *burkqas* and *purdahs*, veils and body-concealing clothing. At the societal-political level, the problems of hunger and poverty in a distant colonized society cannot be solved by intellectual deliberations in the governing circles far away.

The somatic, psychic, and spiritual selves and, on the other hand, external Nature have to be approached very differently from the approach of modern Western psychology and jihadist religious thought. I would suggest that in their place the following four qualities should distinguish our approach.

First is the sense of equality between the somatic, psychic and spiritual selves. The somatic self was never treated as inferior to the psychic or spiritual selves in ancient Hindu scriptures. "The body indeed is the first, original tool of inborn, moral, and ethical duty," say the Hindu scriptures. To treat the human body, the feminine body, or even the body of an animal or plant as something impure and inferior, as some religions and cultures do, is an error that has caused much violence, cruelty, and injustice in human history. Indian traditions teach us to respect the body—whether male or female, human, animal or plant—with respect and nonviolence. Such an attitude has a deep and pervading significance for any culture that hopes to be truly human. Even the concept of the dignity of labor, of physical or bodily work, so dear to Mahatma Gandhi but also to the robust American culture, finds firm roots in the notion of equality of the three individual elements. Extended to include the fourth element, Nature, this notion of equality can lead to an eco-friendly and eco-sound way of living.

Second is the concept of the autonomy of each self and of Nature. The problems of each realm are specific to that realm, with their own history and roots. Hence, solutions to their problems must come from the same realm. An analogous situation from the societal field comes to mind. I am associated with the educational movement named One Teacher School (*Ekal Vidyalaya*) originating in India and now expanding globally. The main philosophy of this movement is that the educational problems and needs of tribal groups or local small communities in remote villages have to be addressed through planning, organization, and execution at the same local, tribal, small-area level. Distant, centralized, remote-controlled planning of the colonial or postcolonial type would not work. The autonomy of the tribal group or the local community has to be respected, understood, and utilized to bring about solutions in education; the life of any order or organization lasts much longer if the order is autonomous and undisturbed.

Third is evolution. No self—somatic, psychic, or spiritual, or Nature with its resources—can take shortcuts to growth or change, but the pathway of each evolving in its own mode is always open, be it at the individual/internal level or at the community/external level. Ancient Indian sages thought of evolution through two central concepts and steps. The first was consistent and focused effort practiced without fears and doubts, a concept re-presented to mankind by the Nobel Laureate poet, Rabindranath Tagore. The second was the concept of *Samskara*, dear to the ancient sages, and one of the important themes of this book. Only through consistent and focused work over a long span of time does evolution of the somatic, psychic or spiritual self become possible. *Samskara* is the outcome of such effort, which may continue over a lifetime and perhaps beyond it. Evolution, understood in this context, might provide an alternative to the Darwinian understanding of evolution in terms of the survival of the fittest, resulting in a pyramidal, hierarchical, and violently cruel picture of Nature and life.

That brings us to the fourth point: no judgment! The pyramidal, hierarchical, colonial way of looking at life, self, and Nature, both inner and outer, results from the insistence on judging others. When the other is treated shabbily as "kaffir" or "Jew," judged fit to be subjected to "the final solution"—mass murder, the most inhuman and satanic cruelty—violence and terrorism take hold of mankind.

On non-judgment, I recall an animal fable in verse written for schoolchildren by a 19th-century Gujarati poet, Dalapatram. The poet described an assembly of animals, where the camel observed that all the other animals had a physical defect of crookedness. The dog had a crooked tail, the elephant had a crooked trunk, the tiger had crooked nails, and so on—it is a long list. All kept quiet but the poem ends with a brief rejoinder by the cunning jackal, who said briefly: "Other animals have each just one thing crooked in their bodies, but, Mr. Camel, in yours all eighteen are so." That simple poem was enough to curb the "holier-than-thou" tendencies in many a pupil in my school.

There is another piece, this one from a well-known writer and philosopher. Joseph Campbell's story is about his visit to a holy man in South India. Talking about the Hindu view of Nature to be divine, Campbell asked the sage point blank how he could justify that Nature was cruel sometimes and creatures of Nature violent? Divinity implies peace, love and tranquility, he argued. The sage's answer was as profound as it was short: "Who are we to judge?" Campbell could not have received a better reply in a shelf-full of books.

I refer to an old Chinese story in this regard. In medieval China, there once lived an old farmer who had a weak, ailing horse for working his field. One day, the sickly horse ran away to the hills. The farmer's neighbors offered their sympathy: "Such rotten luck!" they exclaimed. "Bad luck? Good luck? Who knows?" mused the farmer. A week later, the old horse returned, bringing with it a herd of wild horses from the hills. This time, the neighbors swarmed around the farmer and congratulated him on his good luck. His reply however was the same: "Good luck? Bad luck? Who can tell?"

Sometime later, while trying to tame one of the wild horses, the farmer's only son fell off its back and broke his leg. Everyone thought this was bad luck. "Bad luck? Good luck? I don't know," said the farmer. A few weeks later, the king's army marched into the village and conscripted every able-bodied young man living there. The farmer's son, laid up with a broken leg, was let off, for he was thought to be of no use to them.

Now what was this? Good luck or bad luck? Who can tell?

The old Chinese wisdom is part of the Eastern way of looking at what seem to be opposites and contradictions at first sight. The first sight could lead to conflicts, strife, violence; a second look is necessary.

According to Zen, saying that what is evil includes the good is not to assert that there is no difference between evil and good, just that the traditional dualisms need to be replaced with an understanding of the unity of being. The Zen master Suzuki describes it in this way: All forms of evil must be said somehow to be embodying what is true and good and beautiful, and to be a contribution to the perfection of Reality. To state it more concretely, bad is good, ugly is beautiful, false is true, imperfect is perfect, and also conversely. This is, indeed, the kind of reasoning that brings the God-nature to be immanent in all things.

On matters of detachment, Swami Vivekananda put it in his convincing and compelling way when he attended the World Religion Conference in Chicago: "There is a thorn in my finger and I use another to take the first one out. When I have taken out the first, I throw both of them aside; I have no necessity for keeping the second thorn because both are thorns, after all. So any negative tendencies plaguing our minds have to be counteracted by the good ones. But what do we do after that? Even the good tendencies have now to be restrained." He explains this further: "The idea is to renounce attachment to any ideal—good or bad—and work, but let not the mind be unduly anxious about the results. Let the ripples come and go, let huge actions proceed from us, but let them not make too deep an impression on our souls." He tells us how to be guided by the ancient wisdom and act in the modern world: "Work as if we are a stranger in this land, a sojourner; this is the amount of detachment that is required. Doing the moral and ethical duty, which is ours at any particular time, is the best thing we can do in this world, and such karma is our moral and ethical duty."

Another example of attachment and detachment is experienced by many of us. When I am riding with the owner of an expensive car, I might admire the smoothness of the ride after the car runs over a pothole. However, the owner would be worried that damage might have been done to the car. Another way to learn about detachment is in a statement that the greed of anything, even greed of knowledge, is as undesirable as greed of gold.

From the Psychic Self toward the Philosophic Self

To be happy is one of the most natural objectives of all. Surprisingly, most do not know its how, why and what. If pressed to define happiness, most of us would begin to wonder what it is. Mental happiness is relative and momentary in the realm of the psychic self. The laws of Nature, it should be recognized clearly, also apply to the realm of the psychic self. The psychic self is as much a part of Nature as the somatic self. In Nature at large, Newtonian laws of motion apply. In the natural domain of physics, an object accelerates when an external force is applied. The object stops accelerating and moves at some speed when the force is removed. Similarly, in the psychic domain, as one's desires are fulfilled, one feels "accelerated," happy, in a state of ecstasy. But that state is not lasting and eventually fades when there is no more "acceleration." How to deal with these fluctuations? What is true of happiness and success is also true of unhappiness and failure. How, then, to be happy? What is "happiness"? I would say that a trained mind, a *Samskaric* psychic self, is able to adjust to both success and failure; *Samskara* acts like a filter moderating the effect of both.

A person with a modest existence may be mentally more stable than a person with great wealth. Pain and misery is associated with both extreme poverty and extreme wealth. Rogues and parasites will find a way to be close to extremely wealthy people.

We must dive deeper into the psychic self, not merely through the intellectual tools available to Western science but also through the tools available in Eastern and Indian traditions. But a few words are in order about the Indian tradition. It is very long, extending back many millennia. In the last thousand years of its history, during its "medieval period," people of India allowed their psychic selves to be shattered in the hope of entering into an immortal spiritual self. This obsession with the spiritual self has been responsible for a terrible history of plunder and slavery that became their lot for nearly a millennium.

Vedic sages, in ancient times dating back perhaps to five millennia before the Christian era began, had become obsessed with the spiritual self, when the psychic self was under the assault of great unhappiness. The somatic and psychic selves are always in flux, either toward or away from happiness. The first layer of the somatic self— which is kaleidoscopic, random, and directionless— must not mix with the psychic flux, which is directional and has substratum, bedrock moorings. The psychic self is a go-between, a bridge between the two ends of man's total self, the physical and the metaphysical.

The human species is distinguished through its psychic self. Indian mythology describes the differences in this way. The God of Creation (Brahma) not only created humans, but also demons and angles (gods, kings). Demons lack ethics, compassion, and are totally ruthless and self-centered. A man or an animal in form can be a demon, human, or an angel. His rules of the game were simple. Demons could transform to humans by becoming compassionate (*daya*). Humans could transform to angels by becoming charitable (*dana*). Obviously the receiver of dana, who is desperate to receive some help, would believe the giver must be an angel. And control (*daman*) over desires, implying that the person who has gone through the process of detachment, and subration, has transcended to the highest state of being, that is becoming selfless and full of universal love, could bring a person within the realm of divinity. In short, the three attributes, daya, dana, and daman maintain the separation of the three categories of life in nature and the divine creator Himself.

However our existence is in nature and nature at this point in time has not allowed to populate the earth with only angels.

In matters of governing ourselves, the belief that "good people" would make government itself become an apparatus dedicated to the well-being of its subjects is contradictory, because people who are so altruistic and dedicated would not need government to begin with. Even the framers of the Constitution, a document which is held as a paragon of freedom and yet gave birth to one of the most dangerous centralized governments in the world, understood this fact:

> "If men were angels, no government would be necessary. If angels were to govern men, neither external nor internal controls on government would be necessary. In framing a government which is to be administered by men over men, the great difficulty lies in this: you must first enable the government to control the governed; and in the next place oblige it to control itself."
>
> - James Madison

When might the primary standard, there can be no fixed principles, only the whims of rulers. Any realistic conception of freedom must entail that our institutions, whether political, economic or social, must be constructed and maintained, not on the basis of might, but on the basis of moral principles. The spiritual self is Universal and, depending on what one believes, is everywhere (as All-Pervading *Brahman*) and is associated with all species of living beings—or is nowhere (Ultimate Nothingness or Sunyata). The Vedic sages have not identified the spiritual with the Real (Nature). It was clearly stated that what was wisdom for the spiritual self was ignorance for the other two, namely the somatic and psychic, and vice versa. There was no judgment associated with this. Each self and its wisdom were treated separately, with equal respect and equality. The scriptures warn in non-ambiguous language that, "those who think that the Real is material, are in darkness. But those who think that the Real is spiritual are in greater darkness." Our somatic existence is in natural that is the material world and the psychic self is the bridge; it is not the part of spiritual domain.

In a society, at any given time and place, the good portion of people are confined to the somatic realm, and the rest live in the psychic realm. This should be accepted without passing judgment and without assigning any value to it. These different groups should not fight, but coexist, like patchwork. The image of "a bowl of soup," sometimes offered as an image of a perfect or preferred society, would create problems. Their union will not create brotherhood or equality, but may cause the loss of uniqueness and identity. Mixing the somatic, psychic, and spiritual strata of individuals or society would lead to disharmony, contempt, hatred, and violence. Due processes of sub-ration and evolution have to be undergone, through continuous effort, before one achieves one's identity.

Human nature is not just a matter of heredity, but also responsibility and achievement. There are individuals born as human beings who behave worse than animals. On the other hand, Nature looks to human beings for greater possibilities, not to be explored in contradictions and exploitation but in balance and harmony. The great Indian scientist and botanist J. Bose made a lasting contribution to human knowledge and sensibility when he demonstrated through scientific experiments that Nature, including plants and trees, knows and feels.

The unchanging, absolute truth of the spiritual self can never become the truth of the somatic and psychic selves. In fact, this is poison for the psyche, since the truth of the psyche is relative, changing and pragmatic. Watch out for religious zealots brandishing unchanging, absolute "spiritual" truths, only to build their empires and maintain their power over the masses. Nothing produces as much suffering and degradation for the somatic and psychic selves, individual and social, as mixing the religious absolute with their domains.

Psychological truth is a perpetual process of harmonizing between intellectual and intuitive truths. Pragmatic truth is a changing perception of self-preservation and results from a changing environment. At the pragmatic level, a person and a society adapts to the changing demands of a shifting environment. The objective, if any, is to survive. There is nothing eternal or absolute about this; it comes from the individual's and the society's ability to conform to the supreme law of evolution. It can also be seen as a variation of the economic law of supply and demand. The ability to change and a sense of temporality is the power behind this truth. However, the pragmatic truth and associated actions do not have a purpose and a direction, which brings us to a basic problem.

Pragmatic truth could very well be capable of change, but it cannot forever be temporary. An endlessly temporary truth and an endlessly temporary self would simply not do. It must be conceded that the ever-changing responses of the pragmatic self to the ever-changing demands of a shifting environment are a search for something stable, a march toward the permanent. The psyche must mature to a state that can be reborn into the spiritual self. The processes of sub-ration and transcendence are not processes of a mixed melting pot—they are processes of *Samskara*, hard work and tough love, detachment, gradual transformation, and evolution.

How can this be achieved? My perception is through the loving soul, liberator of the psychic self. It is neither the liberator of the somatic self, nor of the spiritual self, and the reason is clear: the psyche has inherent pride, I-ness. Pride and its evolutes are the constituent components of the psychic self. Pride and intellect are the components that bind its self-importance, its feeling of uniqueness. The moment pride is given up, love springs forth. The journey from being self-centered to selfless is the truest and most worthwhile journey. This is the realm of the philosophic self, a sub-layer of the psychic self at the doorstep of the spiritual self.

Psychic Evolution to the Philosophical Self

Vivekananda described himself by saying that first he was like a stone, inert and inactive. Then he was a mischief-maker, harassing his mother, who had difficulty making him considerate and called him "Satan"—a devil. Indian tradition equates devilishness with ignorance. His transformation was initiated only after his visit to Ram Krishna Paramhansa, recommended by Professor Hasting. His Samskaric family had created an environment that made it easier for him to transcend to his philosophical self. The mind of a youth is less conditioned, with little history. The mind could lean toward devilishness or idealism. However, if preconditions like the environment during the growing-up period are good, the chances are that the mind leans toward idealism; vigor and hope spring to change the social order for the better.

Recall Krishnamurti's teachings. He continually reminded listeners about the conditioned mind. The unconditioned mind, due to the absence of historicity, is able to visualize a reality of goodness, truth and beauty. A conditioned mind, when it sees a dead end, regresses instead of advancing toward the philosophical self. It starts rationalizing and socializing instead of trying to transcend with inspiration and creativity. A practical man can be inhibited against philosophy since he thinks of it as a pursuit of unreality. The path of regression is the path toward bondage and untenable hierarchies, due to man's ignorance of transcendence toward freedom.

The field of philosophy encompasses not only mathematics and science but also the fields of the humanities, including morality, human well-being, rationality, realism, and idealism. The process of transcendence is one of growth. During the growing up period, the child learns to walk and talk and play simple games, employing the somatic and pre-psychic selves. As the child grows up, more human faculties are developed. For example, intellect is needed for science and mathematics. Intuition, feelings, and idealism come along with the intellect. To be in the realm of the philosophic self, every human faculty has to function. The philosophic self is fully developed when every human faculty is integrated, in balance with its opposites, complementing each other, and each pair is in balance with the other pair. The total human self is at the doorstep of the spiritual domain, when every human faculty is in total harmony with all other faculties.

The problem arises when one faculty dominates other faculties. For example, some scientists practice scientific imperialism—the idea that science is capable of answering all questions of human interest. Thomas Kuhn explains that sometimes there is a paradigm shift in science where there is an act of faith, and reason alone could not have rationally compelled the shift.

Science for Kuhn is an intrinsically social activity—the existence of the scientific community, bound together with a shared paradigm, is a prerequisite for the practice of normal science. Kuhn's ideas have brought the concept of cultural relativism into social sciences. The central idea is that there is no such thing as absolute truth. The bottom line is that all human faculties should be in concert, complementing each other to create the beautiful music that the human self is capable of.

Vedic sages wanted psychology to be studied for the removal of dehumanizing power and to free our minds from the momentary pleasures of life. Perpetual regression brings feelings of revenge, exploitation, and therefore bondage. In the realm of the psychic self, the mind needs to disassociate itself from historical compulsion and enter into the realm of pure love and freedom. It is difficult to give up the past since it contains our heritage and culture. However we need not forget the past—it is good to learn from history, but we need not dwell on it. A philosophy of the Universal is needed to pull people out of a negative mindset and teach them about love, truth, and human goodness.

The philosophic self, a sub-layer of the psychic self, is not in the realm of the spiritual self of non-evolving permanence; it is associated with Nature and therefore evolving. The philosophy of exception and exclusivity (such as "My God is the only God") cannot meet the challenge of natural evolution. The subject-object relationship is natural and ingrained in the somatic realm. However, as one transcends from the somatic to the psychic realm, it helps to comprehend "becoming," that is, removing the subject-object distinction. When the psychic self is in balance and harmony, it cleanses the mental faculty of the prejudice of skin color and castes. Man, who has evolved psychologically, derives strength not from the deep historical past, but from the philosophical height. The natural movement is unidirectional toward the proximity of the philosophic mountaintop, based on the natural laws of thermodynamics.

Psychology and philosophy are two different disciplines; the light of philosophy is brighter than that of psychology: The brighter the light, the greater the need for humility. Buddha did not consider his light to be superior to that of the nightingale. He stopped his sermon to let the bird sing the same message of balance and harmony in her melodies. Current problems are due to excessive faith in science and intellectual reasoning and almost none in other human faculties such as intuition, imagination, devotion and love. Joseph Campbell suggested that we need to give space to myths, fantasies, and other human urges to establish democracy within. *Ruta*, the truth of Nature in material form, works in concert with all the mental faculties.

Psychological Self, Philosophy and Power

Another issue comes up at this point—the question of power. Is power a subject for philosophy?

The Shakta philosophers, who succeeded the Vedic thinkers, would say why not? If wisdom and love, which are beyond power, are capable of satisfying the deepest urges of man, why should man still crave power? The philosopher has no choice but to deal with the question of power. Power will always be present, with or without philosophy. It cannot be wished away from man's world. Power controls existence. As Nazism perverted idealism, power perverts philosophy. The lives of most men are affected by power more than by philosophy. There was a period of history in which the people of India became so indifferent to the relationship between culture and power that for them there was hardly any distinction between foreign rule and independence. This went on for many centuries until contact with British rule.

But what is power? There is blind power, which makes everyone behave alike, as in mob frenzy. Power of this kind robs each person of his or her distinctive personality. There are such mobs not only in the streets but also in sophisticated marketplaces. Like a pack of wolves, there are packs of economic traders. A pack of big traders can make the price of a stock tumble or the price of a commodity skyrocket. Such packs have blind power that they use to their advantage. Even today the economic power plays are norm more so than rarity, and the players include institutions and governments for their advantage.

In contrast to mob power, there is the power of the individual. Such individuals are able to see philosophical truth and their personality is cultured. To transform their vision into reality, they use power. Buddha transformed his enlightenment into a code of conduct for the common man, who can empower himself by practicing that code of conduct and can himself achieve enlightenment.

The culturing of power is not the same as a marriage between noble ideas and power; it happens only after the philosophic death of the noble idea. Only then is the idea reborn as power. As long as it remains at the level of power, further evolution of the noble idea stops. Even a noble idea, if it stops at being power, suppresses people, forcing them to follow the idea mechanically. Such power ferments for a span of time and then explodes with violent force. The Romanian and Russian experiences of the modern period provide us with examples of how noble ideas and power together can distort life. Only when a philosopher-king gives up power voluntarily do we have a good example of the relationship of philosophy and power.

I must add that the philosopher-king has to simultaneously give up his contempt of power. Once power takes over and stops the evolutionary process, the reverse movement starts; the process of descent begins and ends, becoming nemesis, unless the philosopher intervenes and intercepts it. Great ideas of liberty, fraternity, and equality became power through great revolutions. That power became corrupted, as can be seen in many revolutions and struggles for freedom and equality around the globe in the past two centuries.

The descent of an American revolution for independence was intercepted by a succession of brilliant philosopher presidents like George Washington and Abraham Lincoln. India lacked such leaders after Gandhi, Patel, and Nehru. It appears that things are changing and philosopher kings have been able to help in the ascent of power toward the nobility of ideas. Philosophy would never enter into a bargain with nemesis to gain power. Its aim is not to gain power for itself but to keep nemesis powerless. To this aim, it sacrifices every desire, every lure, even its life, just as Lincoln and Gandhi did.

Power is always dynamic. It either ascends or descends, but it is hardly at one level. Power (*Shakti*) has been seen in Indian scriptures to be feminine. Philosophic wisdom is masculine. When there is a union of the two, the powerless male becomes powerful and cultureless power becomes cultured.

Power appears in three forms—as nemesis, corrupt Nature, and noble Nature. When corrupt and noble Natures fight, nemesis gains more power. The way to the reformation of a corrupt body politic is not necessarily to clean up the corrupt part, but to strengthen the noble part.

Recall the story of the American Indian elder and his struggle with his inner nature. He emphasized the good within and did not worry about the bad within. Power is empirical; philosophic wisdom is transcendental. In their union, they do not lose their identities, but become aware of the underlying unity between vision and power, thought and action. It is not like a wedding between a man and a woman. Power is feminine, but not a woman. Wisdom is masculine, but not a man. Feminine and masculine are present in all men and all women. Sometimes, an overly masculine philosophical system, like some aspects of Buddhism and Jainism at some periods of their history, ignored the feminine part of the human personality, probably because of a misconception that the feminine is subordinate to the masculine, power subordinate to philosophic thought. During the last 1,000 years in India, power played its own games with arrogant fools and self-seekers and ultimately she destroyed them all to become a spouse of foreign invaders.

So, what is *Shakti*, feminine power? Perhaps the clue to the solution to the riddle of power and its femininity can be found in quantum physics, rather than philosophy. Feminine power, which is energy, is convertible to matter ($E=mc^2$). The Heisenberg principle proves that small atomic particles can appear as matter, like particles, or a pack of energy, that is, waves. Philosophy distrusts power, while quantum physics explains the possibilities of power. Even Albert Einstein, the philosopher-scientist, had difficulties not only in his relationship with women but also in accepting the statistical nature of quantum physics, as can be seen in his famous statement, "God does not play dice."

As an aside, there is a joke that after his death, Einstein met God at the gate of heaven. His first question was to ask God whether the Supreme Being played dice. God responded, "If I did not play dice, don't you think that life would be boring? In every game, every sport that man plays, there is always an element of chance. Don't women play games with men? If there was no diversity and chance in Nature, how would the world stage of William Shakespeare be without diverse actors?" God was referring to Shakespeare's words that the entire world is a stage and every one of us is an actor who enters, plays his part, and leaves at an appropriate time. Only in heaven was Einstein able to satisfy his intellectual curiosity!

Power, matter, energy, space, and time are all finite expressions of Nature. Philosophic wisdom and love are attributes of the infinite. We need not make the finite subordinate to the infinite. Both have equal status before the transcendental.

In reference to Einstein's equation, his assumption that the velocity of light is constant is significant. Every thing in nature is changing and relative. The realm of the Absolute is constant and unchanging. Most traditions, if not all, see light associated with the realm of the Absolute. In essence, light becomes the threshold, the first glimpse of the Absolute. The goal of a philosopher is to transcend to the highest state of being, the spiritual self. The insight here and explained in later chapters is to becoming selfless, egoless, mass-less and light like with no changing attributes. It is amazing that Einstein was able to connect the traditional thought about the Absolute evolved through millennia with his theory of Relativity.

Power and needs can be controlled only through *Samskara*, which alone can integrate power with philosophic wisdom, making the total human self whole, harmonious, and creative. The urge in matter to overpower reason is as strong as the urge in reason to overpower matter.

There has been a popular misconception, at least among men, about the relationship of women, power, and philosophical enlightenment. Because women are supposed to have a predominant feminine component, and because power is not easily related to philosophical enlightenment, women were supposed to be incapable of philosophical enlightenment. Many religions would not accept women as leaders in their sectarian organizations, as bishops, mullahs, or officiating priests. Evolution demands that this view be changed. In the political domain this change has already occurred, as can be seen in the Asian and European theaters of political power. We have seen many women prime ministers—in Sri Lanka, India, Britain, Israel, Iceland, Bangladesh, and Pakistan.

Evolution, however, is a slow process. During human evolution over thousands of years, power has not evolved beyond corruption, deception and secrecy. What Kautilya in India 2,000 years ago, and Machiavelli 500 years ago, taught to their princes and kings, is gospel to politicians, even today. Power can be trained, educated, and cultured only if it searches for light within its own complexities. The hope for power to be cultured is in its feminine aspect. A woman, a loving wife and mother, needs no reason or spiritualism to love her family. Evolution demands that power be awakened into wisdom.

That is where the ancient Indian concept of "dormant" power and the process and techniques of its understanding become relevant. Ancient scriptures call it *"Kundalini."* According to the scriptures, especially of the yoga and Shakta philosophy, kundalini is the residual power sleeping at the root of the spine in the human somatic self. This power lies deeper than all the labyrinths, close to the Absolute. It is neither good nor bad, but devastating if awakened. Modern physics neither accepts nor rejects such a proposition.

This concept of residual power has much significance and many implications for political extremists and religious fundamentalists, since they hold the view that they are the champions and defenders of purity, justice, and righteousness. An apt example of such aroused and devastating power in recent history is Adolf Hitler. It was perhaps the residual power, aroused so fully without receiving *Samskara* training and cultivation, that made Hitler so ruthless in his so-called insistence on Aryan purity and his efficient genocide of millions of Jews. When a terrorist strikes indiscriminately, he is blinded by that abrupt and unprepared arousal of residual power in him toward both history and humanity; he is flung away out of his human faculties and out of the laws of Nature into an infinite source of energy and is in a state of trance. Psychologically, we all occasionally experience a little of the activity of this residual power as rage. A normal person stops there and instinctively realizes that he should not be in such a state of mind.

There are two parallel powers working within us. One is Nature, perceived as sometimes chaotic; the other is pure, extremely strong, residual power. In the scheme of creation, residual power should remain dormant. However, extremists use residual power without any of the elaborate preparation required to wake it up, and this indiscriminate use is, by and large, the root cause of manmade miseries.

We begin childhood in the somatic self. In later years we grow into the psychological self but never get over the somatic lure. The tendency in most of us is to mix up these two levels of existence. The only way out is to transcend from the somatic to the pre-psychic and then the psychic self.

To sum up, four alternatives are presented before man:
• To be a powerless dreamer, a poet of harmony and love;
• To live a corrupt and deceitful low life and obtain corrupt power;
• To live the life of a fanatic and criminal, a nemesis, a retributive power;
• To live a trans-personal life of abstract and pure dormant power.

None of these alternatives fulfill human potential. The right way is to neutralize these four impulses and create a pathway worthy of human beings. But, astonishingly, today we find these four in all societies round the globe.

More on De-conditioning, and the Further Cultivation of Samskara

We are what we think. If we reflect on the conditioning of the mind, we can see that what we think affects our goals, drives, and even desires. Buddhism's fundamental credo that all suffering is caused by desires builds on the belief that what we think makes us what we are. The conditioned mind becomes inflexible and prevents transcendence from the somatic self to higher states of the psychic and philosophical selves. A few examples are worth considering.

• When a fly is trapped in a glass jar for a couple of days, on removing the lid, there is a very high probability that the fly will not escape out of the jar. Why? It has been conditioned to make its space in the glass as its world.

• A gang member in the urban city will often never escape the cycle of violence or life of a gang as long as he remains connected to the environment he is living in—his "turf."

• Over 75 percent of prison inmates in America return to prison when they are released because they are conditioned to living in an incarcerated state.

Human beings become conditioned based on their own limited equipment. We often claim to "believe what we see"—but in reality we actually "see what we believe." Part of the reason for this is historicity, or the burden of the past, often keeping us stuck in old places. We do not need to forget about past memories, but we need to learn from the past not to repeat those same mistakes. An unconditioned, flexible, and agile mind will allow us to keep sub-rating and transcending to a higher level.

A man of good deeds and thoughts attracts people of the same attributes, and vice versa. That is why it is good to surround oneself with positive- thinking people who share one's values and goals. It is easier for man to climb to higher levels, toward the mountaintop, when he sees that the environment and the company of like and similar people are more conducive for that desired purpose and goal.

Based upon available statistics, the largest killer of people in America is not disease but the stress of being unhappy. One of the causes of stress identified is job dissatisfaction. To punctuate this, research states that most heart attacks occur on Monday morning at 9 o'clock. The obvious reason is that it is the first day of the work week, and many people are terrified to start their stressful or unhappy work.

In many ways our historicity and stress and how we deal with it is part of our conditioning. Humans are inherently imitative of others. Like soldiers or athletes trained for battle, those who have been given proper training will most likely endure and survive better than those who have not.

In science and engineering, there is one method to determine the characteristic of a system under study—it is to apply or feed a pulse or "jolt" into the system. The response of the system to the jolt is the output or signature of that system. A good system has the broadest possible response; that is, the output closely resembles the input. A typical sound system is designed to include both—a woofer for good low-frequency sound response and a tweeter for a very high-frequency sound, so that the output of the combined speaker system is able to reproduce the broadband incoming sound.

Individually, each living organism has its own unique signature to an applied jolt. That signature is the characteristic of the organism or is also known as its transfer function or bandwidth. Obviously it is desirable to have the broadest bandwidth in a human being. The higher the mental bandwidth, the more mental agility, and adaptability the person has. A person with the broadest bandwidth would be able to tune in and communicate with most people, but proper mental training is required.

In a given environment, organisms receive a multitude of impulses and jolts. The response of the organism depends on its somatic and psychic nature. A *Samskaric* man who has been educated and trained, but not conditioned, will have the broadest response and ability to tackle the jolts. A multitude of jolts or impulses can make a man of limited "bandwidth" mentally or physically sick. *Samskara*, educational training and experience help to broaden the bandwidth to survive both mentally and physically.

Some jolts can also help a human being. Some studies say we need to have a purpose in life for action, otherwise a human being, like a muscle, begins to atrophy. A good example of a positive jolt is an electric shock given to a person whose heart has stopped functioning. My friend Chris Chapple, professor of theological studies at Loyola Marymount University in Los Angeles, who sends his students abroad, agrees with me that when American students come back from India they are changed for the better since they have received a jolt of Indian experience. They seem to appreciate what they have in America and are better able to comprehend more about life.

I consider myself in particular and Indo-Americans in general, who are exposed to both Indian and American environments, to be very fortunate. We have been exposed to the best of both worlds—the pragmatic and philosophical, the material and spiritual. India provides experiences of a wide spectrum in almost any field—from the economic diversity of poverty and wealth, and changes in climate, to the fields of cultural and religious diversity. Such pairs of opposites as luxury and poverty, modernity and antiquity, gentleness and violence, sensuality and asceticism, the rural and industrial—the extreme contrasts found in India—I suspect cannot be matched anywhere else. Added to the above, the multiplicity of customs, castes, languages, and the ideas and diversity of religions and philosophic systems have profoundly influenced Western scholars such as Schopenhauer, Nietzsche, Emerson, and Whitman.

Indeed, joining hands or complementing the USA with India reflects part of the natural world, like the north and south of a magnet. Using a magnet as an example, India and the U.S. represent the two ends. Interestingly, the U.S. and India are also almost exactly opposite each other in terms of time zones—12.5 hours ahead or behind. Integrating material and pragmatic America with philosophical and spiritual India, I believe, is good for humanity and the whole world, and it could ultimately lead humanity to transcend to a higher level.

The Journey from Being Self-Centered (Aham) to Selfless (Aum)

In the relationships between India and America, there is an area where both cultures are able to interact symbiotically. The following quotation from Emerson presents a view of life leading in that direction:

"To laugh often and much, to win the respect of intelligent people and the affection of children, to earn the appreciation of honest critics and endure the betrayal of false friends, to appreciate beauty, to find the best in others, to leave the world a bit better, whether by a healthy child, a garden patch...to know even one life has breathed easier because you have lived: This is to have succeeded!"

To define success in these terms is to look at life differently. The difference depicted by Emerson, who, as one of the "transcendentalist" thinkers of America had his roots in Indian Vedantic thought, was grasped by ancient Indian sages to describe a self-centered person with arrogance (I-ness) and *Aum*, the symbol of transcendental Reality.

Aum is *Nirvana*, freedom. Self-centeredness with arrogance is sometimes explained as self-respect, which it is not. It is significant that the discoverers of the Indian scriptures have not attached any names to them; to them, names were not important. In fact, to give any name

TRANSCENDENCE: SAVING US FROM OURSELLVES

as "writer" of the scriptures, let alone as "author," would have been unthinkable for these sages. Lesser Brahmins, though, did have a problem of ego. And the empire-building captains of the Western powers had a similar problem. I believe that the links between East and West were broken by those builders of empires, but there was a major link between the two. It has been said by some historians of early Christianity that Jesus Christ had probably traveled to many places away from his birthplace and that one was India. But later empire builders caused much harm and created false history that deprived people of some countries, including India and other developing nations, of their necessities and their future, and people of other nations of their roots and their past. Also, it produced fatal self-centeredness in individuals and groups against the greater good.

On the one hand is the logic of giving; on the other hand, the relentless process of self-centeredness. On the one hand *Aum*, on the other *Aham*. Such forces as Nazism and terrorism are results of the latter. I am not pleading for the total human self in isolation. Commerce and trade are good, actually beneficial. But helping yourself at the expense of others, knowingly, is not good.

At a glance, we might see the domains of *Aum* and *Aham* side by side, as follows:

Aum: Eternal-Universal, God, Goodness, Love, For All.

Aham: Arrogance, Devil, Evil, Hate, For Me.

Aham or self-centeredness produces distorted forms of domination. On the other hand, participation and sharing creates harmony.

Under the spell of *Aham*, ignorance and self-centeredness, both the ruler and the ruled, the exploiters and exploited, have begun to take a single position—extremism. Instead of being close to the middle ground in human interaction, whether personal, familial, economic, religious or political, many have transgressed the boundaries or borders. Boundaries are a series of barriers that should not be crossed until one has been prepared fully through the processes of sub-ration, evolution and

68

transcendence. Until then, it is best for the majority of people to remain away from borders and not take extremist positions. Extremism is a black hole that exists in every field and domain. Even in such personal activities as eating, extremism can lead to obesity and eventual death. In the economy, extremism leads to an inflation-deflation cycle that spells misery for people. In the field of knowledge, the term "extreme knowledge" was used in the ancient Indian epic, *Mahabharata*. The youngest of the five princes, Sahadeva, was a man of extreme knowledge, with a gift enabling him to look into the future. However, the gift was a curse, because Sahadeva could not prevent his eldest brother, King Yudhisthira, from gambling away his kingdom and dishonoring the queen. His extreme knowledge caused him only pain. The myth of Sahadeva seems to be similar to the myth of Cassandra, the Trojan princess who also was blessed with the gift of prophecy and burdened by the curse that prevented any one from ever believing her.

But evolution makes extremism relative and changing. Senator Goldwater's statement that "Extremism in the defense of the country is no vice, and the pursuit of moderation is no virtue" was an extremist's statement in the year 1964. He was handily defeated due to such statements. But today, after 9/11, such a stand might be more acceptable to a nation hurt by that tragedy. The laws of evolution and change apply in all domains.

Chapter 4

The Interaction of Nature and the Total Human Self

Autonomous yet Interacting Units

We urgently need to understand the depth of our relationship to Nature. Observation of the complexity and richness of our total human self compels us to view it as a multi-layered entity, with each domain autonomous but interconnected. There is no single, fixed border between the somatic and psychic selves or the psychic and spiritual selves. Instead, there are a series of boundaries, grey areas, between each domain, and these must be approached with the utmost care and full preparation, or such an approach could be fatal. It is usually better for the majority of us to remain close to the center, away from the periphery. Only a snake charmer who has prepared himself for his profession can be close to a snake.

The total human self is very much a part of Nature, as are the layers of selves. Of these, the somatic self, which contains all the parts of our body, such as the heart and brain, is closest to Nature. But what is Nature? Nature is both matter and energy existing in a continuum of space and time. The psychic self, though it is within the continuum of space and time, has no material aspect; in fact, it is in a sub-space of consciousness.

After the discovery of what we know as Newtonian dynamics, scientists believed in the primacy of matter over mind. However, the direction of dominance reversed after the discovery of quantum physics. Many scientists and philosophers accepted the primacy of mind over matter, a view that has been dominant in India from ancient times. The *Upanishads* stated clearly and emphatically that the life force is a primary reality over non-living matter. The Newtonian/Cartesian dichotomy, elevating matter, has been thus rejected in the Eastern perception.

The debate between those who profess the supremacy of matter and those who perceive the supremacy of mind has, however, enriched our understanding of the relationship of and interactions between the total self (with its many layers) and Nature. On the one hand, Professor Hiriyanna states: "Everything that exists is either Life Force or for Life Force." On the other hand, the Anthropic Principle stated by the British physicist Brandon Carter in the 1970s stated: "If some feature of Nature is required in the natural world for our existence, then it must indeed be the case." Another statement, "Only things that can be known are those compatible with the existence of the knowers," has essentially the same meaning.

It is no wonder, then, that the riddle of all riddles for a scientist is the inter-relationship of brain and mind. Even more incomprehensible is that one mind can comprehend another mind, though the two are separate and totally isolated from one another. The question then is: Are we so isolated? The *Vedanta* would not accept "yes" for an answer. "All living souls are connected with the gale of the sun," says Ananda Koomarswami. J. Krishnamurti speaks of our mind being connected with the Universal Mind. We have come a long way toward recognizing our interconnectedness as stated in chapter one.

Organisms, Nature and Her Wealth

An ancient Sanskrit saying, "Wealth resides in the seas," also implies that wealth resides in every other form of Nature. Gold and diamonds, wheat and rice, metal and minerals, pearls and fish, fruits and herbs—the bounty is unlimited. There is enough in Nature for everyone's needs, though not for everyone's greed, as Mahatma Gandhi astutely observed. How does one gain this wealth without violating Nature or our own selves? The answer is found in the wisdom of the Vedic sages.

We know that we are connected to and symbiotic with Nature. We are neither external to it, entering Nature from outside to conquer it; nor are we prisoners within it, trapped and striving to get out and escape into some sort of liberated state. This is important because the ancient wisdom teaches us to live fully before attempting to achieve *Nirvana*. Life fulfills itself within Nature through a ceaseless process of growth and evolution, which progresses in two directions, internal and external. Internal evolution, focused on the psyche, has been explored more fully in Eastern wisdom. External evolution, focused on Nature, has been explored more fully in the Western sciences. Both are equally important, because without one we cannot achieve the other—such are the strength and reality of the inter-relationships and interactions between Nature and our total human self.

Organisms, by which are meant all living creatures, are self-organizing systems. In the process of metabolism, there is a continuous exchange of energy and matter, renewal and recycling. When organisms experience self-renewal, through birth, death and rebirth, they develop to a higher level or, in other words, they evolve in a process of self-maintenance and self-transcendence. When an organism is dissected to gain knowledge about it, the organism loses its properties and characteristics as a system, and is destroyed as an organism.

Systems are dynamic and thermodynamic—dynamic because they are active and there is a continuous exchange of matter and energy, thermodynamic because they degrade with respect to time. They operate in two ways—linearly, but often non-linearly, and between the two extremes. In the Western sciences, knowledge of Nature has been gained through dissection, division and analysis, described as a reductionist approach.

The Eastern holistic view, on the other hand, grew through harmony, synthesis and integration. These views, Western and Eastern, based on analysis and synthesis, seem contradictory. In reality, they form a pair of opposites and they complement each other. Both are required in order for man to have a more complete relationship with Nature. Analysis and synthesis, reductionism and holism—each pair of opposites is complementary; one cannot exist without the other, as in the case of a magnet. Nature's favorite game is to create pairs of opposites.

It is important to note that self-organizing systems, or living organisms, are autonomous. They determine their own structure, function and size. They determine their own interaction with the environment, and they also have freedom of choice. Though there is freedom, actions are controlled by such collective activities as praise, blame, reward, punishment, values, ethics, legal codes, guilt and gratitude. Freedom in its purest form together with *Samskara* results in the highest form of creativity.

Table 4-1

	Psyche (mind)	Brain (matter)
Existence, substance	Conscious space with thoughts, feelings, pain, pleasure, purpose, goal, why and why not	Matter, nerves, chemicals, atoms and sub-atomic particles like electrons, nuclei, neurons
Activities, functions	Subjective, participates, becoming, all within, introspective, private, chooser, involved in larger thermodynamic, irreversible processes of evolution; Heisenberg's principle of uncertainty and Schrodinger's probability applies (thermodynamic)	Objective, observer (Shakshi) and observable by others (public) being; brain can retrieve and go back in past that is reversible in time, like tracing back planetary orbits (dynamic)
Diversity and unity	Individual mind/psyche is unique and distinguishable	All electron/atoms cannot be distinguished from one another

Detection, investigator	Act of investigation of thought process will disturb the process; observer and observed cannot be the same	Act of detection of orbiting electron will disturb the state to be detected since the energy required to detect is comparable or larger than the energy of a quantum jump
Mind/brain interaction, unifying and uplifting	Need cultivation of somatic self (Samskara) that helps to bring self in proper frame of mind and to the path of the higher levels of psychological and philosophical self and possibly to a state of blissful mind	Curious mind, with extraordinary brain makes an individual a good scientist to discovering the multifaceted truth of nature—experiencing flashes of the blissful mind.
Indivisible process	Thoughts jump from one to the next; they are indivisible, non-continuous, and un-analyzable; there is no fractional thought in a conscious mind.	Electrons jump orbit to orbit when they acquire or lose energy, also known as a quantum jump. The process is non-continuous, expressed in unity, and cannot be analyzed or visualized.

In the Eastern view, the freedom to choose—free will—is relative, limited and illusory, not absolute. Though we are free, we do not live in isolation. This is an all-important distinction, between freedom and isolation. Eastern wisdom tells us that we are embedded in the cosmos and are an inseparable part of it, with the objective to shed ego-sensation and merge with the totality.

Mind, Matter, and Nature

The method of analysis, which marks the Western sciences, has separated mind from matter. According to it, only organisms have mind. But the Eastern view, based on synthesis, points out that both mind and matter are two aspects of the same phenomenon. The eminent scientist Dr. Kothari has compared the non-material mind with the material brain, as shown in *Table 4-1*. We can see differences and similarities between the mind and brain. Quantum physics has brought mind and matter closer to the unity perceived by the ancient seers. A directive from the findings of Dr. Kothari is that we need to grow in both directions, internal and external.

The question here is how to perceive the mind itself. The Eastern view would argue that there are different levels of mind based on different levels of development. In a broad sense, consciousness and self-awareness are interchangeable. Awareness is a property of mentation at any level of a living organism, from single cells to a highly complex multicultural organism like a human being. But self-awareness emerges fully only in human beings.

The Western view in the past considered matter to be primary and argued that consciousness was a property of complex material patterns that emerge only at a certain stage of biological evolution. The Eastern view is quite opposite. It considers mind to be primary. In the Eastern view, consciousness is non-material, formless, timeless, and void of all content. Such a state has been described differently, using words such as "Pure Consciousness," "Ultimate Reality," "Suchness," "Field of Intelligence," and "Universal Mind." This manifestation of consciousness is associated with the divine in Eastern spiritual traditions. All forms of matter and organisms are seen as patterns of divine consciousness. This mystical view of consciousness is based on the experience of reality in a non-ordinary mode of awareness achieved through meditation.

The scientific and mystical views seem completely opposed to each other. We are, then, required to choose either the scientific or mystical in our view of matter and consciousness and their relationship; either to accept the primacy of matter or the primacy of mind; either to see consciousness emerging out of matter or to see matter produced within the larger consciousness.

However, the systems view of mind seems to be perfectly consistent with both the scientific and the mystical view of consciousness, providing an ideal framework for unifying these two views. It makes clear that the new vision of reality is also an ecological vision. Thus the scientific vision based on reason and analysis and intuitive awareness forms a concept of oneness for all life—an interdependence symbiotic to the nature of human existence. Through the systems view of mind, the individual feels connected to the cosmos as a whole. It becomes apparent that ecological awareness is truly spiritual. By binding ourselves with Nature, we are connecting to a nearly 5,000-year-old belief based on Indian Vedic scriptures as well as other traditions, which include the cultures of the Incas and the Aztecs of the Americas. Being linked to the cosmos is expressed in the Latin root of the word "religion" or "religare," which means to bind strongly, as well as in the Sanskrit word "yoga," which means "union." The parallels between science and mysticism are extended not only to modern physics but also to biology and psychology with equal justification.

To sum up this discussion on different views of Nature, I focus on two major options, two kinds of natural orders: Heraclitean and Pythagorean. The former is more Eastern and the latter is more Western, similar to the Laplacian and Newtonian views.

The *Heraclitean view* states:

• There is a time-bound evolution of structures, and the rise of order from chaos, followed by a slow decay.

• Order is nonpermanent and spontaneous, it decays. Nature is running down in energy, but running up organizationally, with ever more information, wisdom, finer arts, and so on.

• Because Nature is running down in energy, it follows that there is an end state. The end state of order is chaos, anarchy, maximum entropy, zero information, and all noise, producing maximum randomness and disorder.

Opposed to the Heraclitean view is the *Pythagorean view*, with three counterpoints:

• There is a timeless, unchanging order of things. This can best be seen in mathematics and Newtonian physics.

• As opposed to the spontaneous order and decay of the first view, this second view stresses the orderliness of crystals, of atomic and planetary motions. This perception implies the twin notions of permanence and reversibility in time. It is a deterministic vision, leading Laplace to claim that given the initial conditions, the state of the universe can be accurately determined at any given point of time.

• This also implies zero decay, infinite order, infinite wisdom, and a corresponding conception of God.

The strong cosmological principle states that the initial state of the universe was totally chaotic, implying maximum entropy, zero information, and maximum disorder. This is the single most important reason that destroys the idea of the clockwork universe of Laplace and Newton.

These two views of natural order lead me to the following additional observations:

• Order occurs from total chaos. The initial condition of the universe, born out of chaos, is not known. Idealists believe it is only God's knowledge.

• There are many diverse orders, including organisms, but only one chaos.

• For longevity to occur, any order or organism requires its own autonomy to slow down the process of decay. The life of the order is even longer if it has learned to adapt to its environment.

• Mixing of orders accelerates decay. The implication is that the somatic, psychic or spiritual should not be mixed with each other, and the autonomy of every order, every self, should be maintained. The freedom to choose, free enterprise, and freedom in general should never be given away or lost.

• Old orders decay and die; newer orders are generated. In other words, species rise and disappear. Empires rise and fall.

• Absolute determinism is gone forever in a chaotic universe, since the initial condition of the cosmos is not known. All processes, including measurements, are irreversible.

• Outcomes in Nature are never 100 percent certain. Nature is un-predictable.

• Astronomers accept galactic expansion. Expansion is common in the human psyche. Outward knowledge of Nature is accelerating, thanks to the technology of computers and the Internet.

• The creative order-generating activity of the human mind is at least as important as Nature's evolutionary processes, perhaps more important. It is interesting to note that Nature's evolutionary processes, in fact, gave birth to the human body, its somatic self, and the psyche, which itself is capable of generating orders. This is analogous to a light source like the sun and a pinhole that becomes a source but is still dependent on the original light source.

• There are two human evolutions—biological and cultural. The results of cultural evolution are less diverse than those of biological evolution. Biological evolution is more complex, more diverse, and takes more time to accomplish results. Cultural evolution takes a much shorter time.

• Biological or somatic evolution is natural, and therefore is un-predictable and "blind." The implication is that somatic evolution is not accessible to the human mind.

I now make a connection of the total self with Nature in this way: If the somatic self has two components, genetics and the body, then the information of the initial condition of a process that creates order is the genetics of the order. Humanity, I suspect, can never have knowledge of the genetics of the universe. Unification in general and unification of the four forces in particular, cannot be realized only through reductionist intellectual pursuit, in spite of advances made in the string theory. Unification apparently is possible only by employing the system's approach. The implication is that every human faculty, every layer and sub-layer of the total human self, should work in harmony with each other to realize unification, which may be possible through the experience of becoming selfless, losing the identity of the self that has unified with God's nature.

On the question of inward expansion, I believe that progress of the total human self is quite slow. We need to put more resources at work to have rapid inward expansion, taking forward the works of the ancient Indian thinkers. My intuition tells me that the only way to discover Nature is to discover our own selves through introspection. Humanity needs to find its own multidimensional space and go beyond somatic and psychological space. We seem to use mostly intellect and hardly any other faculty, like the intuitive mind.

Samskara – Self in Sync with Itself; Ruta – Cosmic Order

The sages and masters of ancient Indian culture have given us two words, two concepts, two perceptions—twin keys to peace and prosperity. These keys, *Samskara* and *Ruta*, if turned in synchrony, open the gates to the wonderful worlds of health, wealth and wisdom.

What *Samskara* is for the self, *Ruta* is for the universe and for Nature; they are both order-enhancing forces. To understand *Ruta*, the cosmic order, the profound rhythm of Nature and of the human body, we might begin by paying attention to the great movements of the sun, the moon, and the countless stars; of the circles of the seasons; the cycles of seed-flower-fruit-seed in each and every plant, shrub and tree, from the banyan trees of India to the redwoods of California. In the beating of the heart, the pulses of the blood, the marvels of the human body, we begin to understand the independence and harmonies given us by *Samskara*.

This interaction can be harmonious and productive only through *Ruta*, the essence of Nature, and *Samskara*, the essence of self. Order and harmony due to *Ruta* in the mega-world of Nature and *Samskara* in the macro-world of the individual self, together provide a sound foundation, making it possible to initiate processes that lead toward *Nirvana*.

Ruta also operates at the micro-world level; it is the Samskara of the quantum physicists that helped us discover and understand the operation of the micro-world.

Nature, Survival through Coexistence, and the 80/20 Rule

As stated earlier, the favorite sport of Nature is to create pairs of opposites for the purpose of their mutual survival. The 80/20 principle shows how survival through the coexistence of opposites becomes possible.

Adi Shankara, 12 centuries ago, advised us that to learn more about a nemesis, the learner should become one. This advice implies that a nemesis is the opposition or competition, not necessarily an enemy to destroy. Shankara's comment tells us that a pair of opposites must learn to coexist in harmony and complement each other for the greater good. Living organisms coexist in multidimensional space to survive. Multiple pairs of opposites constitute multidimensional space. In an unpredictable Nature, multiple pairs of opposites must exist to maintain life. Elements of a pair of opposites cannot be separated, any more than the north pole of a magnet can be separated from the South Pole. Ancient Vedic teachers would say that these two opposites need to complement each other instead of being at war so that they can coexist in balance and harmony.

In a similar way, organisms must not only coexist to survive but at locations away from multiple boundaries. This is because organisms perish if they hit a boundary. It is safest to be in the center of a multidimensional space, although it may not be as rewarding in the center. A zebra remaining in the center of the herd is probably safest from an attack by a predator; however, this animal may not have access to the freshest grass. A presidential candidate almost always claims to be at the center to increase the likelihood of getting elected. President Obama succeeded by projecting himself as being close to the center though his record showed that he was more to the left.

Just as it is painful and miserable to be extremely poor, I suspect it would be painful to be extremely rich, due to being self-centered, distrustful, and always afraid of losing wealth.

However, a boundary can be approached if proper preparations are undertaken and completed by the one who goes close to it. A Nepalese Gurkha, for example, can exist at a high altitude because he is acclimatized to that height, having been born there. But a man from the plains, without adequate preparation, would sicken at that altitude and might die. Similarly, every organism has a unique location in multidimensional space. A snake charmer or lion tamer survive and prosper near a venomous snake or man-eating animal, perceived as dangers by others.

Boundaries of multidimensional space are dynamic and move in the course of time. During the growing-up process, the boundaries around the child move away as the child becomes more capable, enlarging the living space around him. However, as we age and come closer to our demise, the boundaries around us come closer, shrinking the living space. Sooner or later we will hit the boundary or the boundary will hit us causing our demise, but one should never be afraid of it. Boundaries are not fine lines of demarcation; they are "grey" areas of "in between" combined often with a series of obstacles that one needs to break through and overcome for true growth. Boundaries can also be thought of as black holes or death traps.

We can reflect on the principle of the 80/20 rule that constitutes many examples of opposites coexisting. The 80/20 principle states that 80 percent of a task is relatively easy and can be done in 20 percent of the time; the remaining 20 percent of the task is difficult and can take the remaining 80 percent of the time. The 80/20 principle also implies that work gets harder as one approaches 100 percent of the task. As an example, we can visualize a series of barriers, with each succeeding barrier getting higher and harder to cross. The Japanese consider the number eight to be good and close enough to being successful, and to attain the level of eight is admirable for them because the number ten is perfection, meant only for gods. Indian tradition considers number nine close enough for perfection.

The pattern of the 80/20 principle was first discovered in 1897 by Italian economist Vilfredo Pareto. Living in 19th-century England, Pareto found that most wealth and income in Britain went to a small minority of the people. The 80/20 principle was discovered again by Harvard professor George Zipf in 1944 and called the Principle of Least Effort. There are numerous examples of the 80/20 phenomenon in our lives. For example, 20 percent of Motorists cause 80 percent of accidents; 20 percent of those who get married comprise 80 percent of the divorce statistics. This last calculation implies that the statistic of a 40 percent divorce rate in America (four out of ten) is actually deceiving. More accurate data would be that two couples out of ten get divorced, not once, but twice, making the divorce rate not really 20 percent but 40 percent.

The proportion of 80/20 is not exact but a symbol of distribution; it could be 60/40 or 90/10 or in-between. The 80/20 principle shows how the majority of something coexists with its opposite, the minority. What is clear is that one does not see a linear or balanced pair of 50/50 as often in life as non-linear unbalanced pairs of opposites. Hindsight is always 20/20, but the result is mostly 80/20. The theory of chaos and the 80/20 principle describe the universe as unbalanced or non-linear. The ancient Vedic teachers saw that the ordered universe was created out of its opposite, chaos, making it obvious that these two realms ultimately had to coexist. Physicist Stephen Hawking now concedes that there may not have been a Big Bang for the creation of the universe, since it implies singularities that we have not experienced in Nature, the implication being that there may be cycles of creation and destruction as suggested in the *Vedas*.

The metaphor for the cosmic dance of creation and destruction found its most profound expression in the Hindu god Shiva, also known as Nataraja. Fritjof Capra, in his book *The Tao of Physics*, compares this cyclical dance of creation and destruction with dancing atomic and sub-atomic particles, and quotes Ananda Coomaraswamy:

"In the night of *Brahman*, Nature is inert, and cannot dance till Shiva wills it: He rises from His rapture, and dancing sends through inert matter pulsing waves of awakening sound, and lo! Matter also dances; He sustains its manifold phenomena. In the fullness of time, still dancing, He destroys all forms and names by fire and gives new rest. This is poetry, but none the less science."

Dancing Shiva symbolizes not only the cosmic cycles of creation and destruction, but also the daily rhythms of birth and death that are seen as the basis of all natural existence.

One of the most dramatic examples of the 80/20 principle at work is with films. Two economists working for an entertainment corporation found that four films (representing 1.3 percent out of 300 produced films in a period of 18 months) returned 80 percent of the total box office revenue; the other 296 films (98.7 percent) earned only 20 percent. The 80/20 principle is employed by many organizations to assist people to efficiently maintain their resources and to increase productivity. The 80/20 principle, a law of Nature, can also be used in the somatic and psychic realms to obtain the desired goals of life. As the somatic and psychic selves are part of Nature, the 80/20 principle can expedite the process of transcendence.

The 80/20 principle is applicable not just for an individual but also for a project, an organization, and for the whole of humanity. On a simple project level, one can use the 80/20 principle while reading a book. Try reading first the book's conclusion, then its introduction, and then its conclusion again. Then dip lightly into whatever else is important, instead of reading the whole book from cover to cover.

One can learn to use leverage—for example, of time, effort and capital—as 20 percent of a project, property or company, to improve, own or control 80 percent of the profits. Working for someone else or a corporation in most cases is not going to make one wealthy unless the employer is exceptionally generous. Investing in real estate income properties is what helps many acquire wealth by leveraging capital using the 80/20 principle. Time and effort can be leveraged by employing people for a project. The corporate owner or CEO of a company leverages his time and makes his fortune by employing more people. Capitalism and free enterprise, the essence of the 80/20 principle, is one of the most natural and efficient economic systems. As a system, it also adapts better to a changing environment compared to any other, including communism and socialism. The reason China is doing better economically, in spite of being a communist country in name, is due to the fact that it has adopted many of the capitalist tools. Any system that motivates, guides, and encourages its entire people to work hard and uplift their lives with minimum government hindrance is bound to succeed. A full creative force is another reason for the success of the free enterprise system. A poem by Neil Pert explains clearly what could happen if a forced equality (socialism) were to prevail over Nature.

The Trees

There is unrest in the forest
There is trouble with the trees
For the maples want more sunlight
And the oaks ignore their pleas

The trouble with maples
(And they're quite convinced they're right)
They say the oaks are just too lofty
And they grab up all the light
But the oaks can't help their feelings
If they like the way they're made

And they wonder why the maples
Can't be happy in their shade?

There is trouble in the forest
And the creatures have all fled
As the maples scream "oppression!"
And the oaks just shake their heads

So the maples formed a union
And demanded equal rights
The oaks are just too greedy
We will make them give us light
Now there's no more oak oppression
For they passed a noble law
And the trees are all kept equal
By hatchet,
Axe,
And saw…

Other examples of the 80/20 principle in life are selective though not exhaustive. We use this principle when we delegate or outsource, or employ others rather than being employed. Delegating work often helps minimize mental stress. I recommend being a contrarian (20 percent of the whole) rather than being part of the herd (the other 80 percent); in other words, avoid the herd mentality. Students can employ the application of 80/20 in an examination. First go for the "slam dunk" questions to answer (80 percent of the test), then tackle the progressively harder questions (the remaining 20 percent). Answering the easier questions also helps one gain confidence. Make probability work in your favor—it is easier to hit a single or a double (80 percent of the time) than a home run or a "sixer" in cricket (20 percent of the time).

Samskara and the 80/20 principle can be instituted in the realm of education. *Samskaric* education is second only to satisfying the natural somatic needs of hunger; education is the most important nutrient to uplift society. I can think of a few applications of the 80/20 principle for selecting the most relevant levers to help educate students more efficiently. One would be to provide education for the majority of students based on aptitude and attitude. We can establish a competitive spirit in teachers and schools and if we do that, the majority of schools will succeed in giving good education to students. There should be better interaction between students, teachers and parents. And we should use computers, the Internet, and high technology in our classrooms.

In short, pairs of opposites must coexist for survival. Using the 80/20 principle found in Nature, we can make a better world and aid our own survival as human beings. A marriage of a man and woman is probably the most universally understood example of opposites coexisting, and from it comes society's fabric. The husband and wife, two opposite sexes, must learn to coexist and thrive in marriage. They must learn to complement each other and not compete, as though one is the nemesis of the other. If they successfully do so, they will most likely have a successful life with loving and successful children. If parents do not coexist successfully, their children will suffer and bring those scars back into society. As India's imminent physicist J. Bose says, "Learn, respect, and love Nature—Nature probably will help put you on the right path of life."

On Sub-ration and Evolution

What is sub-ration? It is a mental process that helps to rectify errors of judgment. Sub-ration requires rejection of an object, a person, or an idea of a lesser value to accept something of a higher value. Detachment being the prerequisite to sub-ration, sub-ration is a process to reject the stuff of lower values and explore the stuff of higher values.

Sub-ration is the technology of growth and a prerequisite to transcendence, which alone can bridge the distance between clustering and evolution and lead to liberation and harmony. Let us see how it can be done.

The domain of daily life is the best place to see how the process of participation works. Want to avoid problems with your wife and kids and close ones? Keep them busy! That is what we heard from the *rishis* during our college days. How true it is! Change the frequency of confrontation to the frequency of participation. Most human problems originate in miscommunication. What is a miscommunication? It is not so much no-communication as garbled-up communication. In it the transmission frequency and the reception frequency do not quite match each other. The well-known story of the blind men and the elephant shows how miscommunication occurs when what is transmitted (the total reality of the body of the elephant) and what is perceived (only a part, like the tail or the leg or the ear of the elephant touched by one of the blind men) do not match. We have two choices: either get involved in the reverberations of incoherent dialogues (like the talk among the blind men, each insisting that the elephant is what he has chanced to touch—like a thin rope, a thick pillar, a large hand-fan) or get involved in a process of sub-ration. "Get involved—with detachment" is the phrase; "participation" is the word. Recall the words of the *Gita*: Do your ethical and moral duty, without expecting a reward.

This brings us to the second of the three processes, namely, evolution. To start with, we could discuss two types of evolution: somatic and cultural. Somatic evolution is, as we have seen, unpredictable and beyond the scope of understanding by human intelligence.

Cultural evolution is associated with the human mind, that is, the psychic self and self-awareness. Therefore it is visible. It is, for the same reason, foreseeable and predictable. Tools like mathematics, language and science have been used to cultivate self-awareness and to foresee trends in the cultural evolution of mankind and its different societies.

These tools are themselves evolving; some of the most recent and powerful tools include software and hardware technology.

However, these tools are only one part of the story of cultural evolution. The second, perhaps the more important, aspect is the choices made by groups, communities, societies and nations. Cultural evolution depends on such choices. Tools are used; action is taken on the basis of the choices made, goals desired, and values held dear. Then single or multiple "feedback loops" control the outcome.

Gandhi's Spirituality: Many Paths to the Mountaintop

To achieve Ultimate Freedom is to go through a process of many lifetimes—reincarnations, as the scriptures say—and Mahatma Gandhi accepted it in its entirety. Vedanta says that this involves a merging of the individual soul, *Atman*, into the Universal Soul, *Paramatman* or *Brahman*. "*Tat tvam asi*," "Thou art That," says the *Upanishadic* sage. Meditation, good deeds, and performance of the highest duties, good karma and dharma are the instruments available to achieve Godhood, that is, release of all bondage.

Mahatma Gandhi embraced the Jain theory of the many-sidedness of truth, hence the necessity for open mindedness and soul searching. Gandhi believed in egolessness as the highest personal virtue, and was a believer in the brotherhood of man. One can prove with simple arithmetic that every person is at least a 33rd cousin of any other human being. The logic is that a person has two parents, four grandparents and so on, implying that the population doubles every generation. If we go backward in time and multiply the number two 33 times, the number is about eight billion, close to the total human population in this world. His belief in interconnectedness implies that politics cannot be separated from spiritual values, thus leading him in his quest to rectify political injustice.

Gandhi was a believer in the equality of religion. The essence of all religions is to seek ethical action based on self-surrender. His prayer meetings always included recitations from many different religions with a common message, stating that the essence is only one, though the approaches may differ.

In the material world, the objective is to merge with all that exists, like undistinguishable carbon atoms in the diamond. The process involved is to spread from one's own limited body to whatever it comes in contact with. That involves the power of sympathy that sages like Buddha and Christ had. The key is to feel another person's pain and pleasure.

Philosophical freedom and its outcome differ, but surprisingly very little. Overall they seem to complement more than they conflict.

Truth, Universal Love, Ultimate Reality, *Brahman*, God, *Nirvana*— we have heard these words and been inspired, puzzled, enlightened, or put off by them at different times, according to our *Samskaras*. Whatever *It* is called, *It* resides at the mountaintop and we are in the foothills or on the way, at different stages, on different trails. There are many paths to the mountaintop and each one is unique.

All paths and fields of endeavor should be looked at without bias. With love, compassion and freedom for all, we can experience beauty in unbounded space where the boundary between "I" and "Nature" dissolves. You may change the path and go around the obstacles, so long as the direction is toward the mountaintop, where all paths meet.

Dialogue with a Scientist-President/Philosopher-King

During a visit to India, I had the honor of meeting India's brilliant and profound president, A. P. J. Abdul Kalam. I had given him a collection of my articles. I never expected even a formal receipt. However, when I returned to Los Angeles, there was an email from President Kalam.

"Dear Navinji—Thanks for giving me your book, *Lakshmi and Saraswathi* (Goddess of Wealth and Goddess of Wisdom). I am really moved by your last paragraph of the article on 'Gandhi's Spirituality': 'You may change the path to go around the obstacles, so long as the direction is toward the mountaintop, where all paths meet.'—Beautiful and enchanting. Greetings and best wishes.

A. P. J. Abdul Kalam"

I was touched and moved. Not only because the president of India had written to me, but because, in that email, I saw one of the greatest Indian leaders of a profound, ancient culture, who knew the power of *Atman*, as well as one of the greatest Indian scientists, who knew the power of the Atom, meet, with me as a humble witness.

Reading the complimentary words from the president of India several times, I realized the importance of his quote taken from my article on Gandhi's spirituality. I also thought of the president's statement from one of his speeches, that humanity needs to transcend from the rigidity of religions to the freedom and openness of spirituality. How do we do it? First and foremost, we must emphasize the positive aspects of every tradition and belief system and reject negative degrading statements like, "My God is the only true God," or "I am holier than thou." Such statements imply regression going in a historicity of past prejudice that could bring actions of revenge. Such beliefs have no place in the path of transcendence. As stated earlier, it is important to be non-judgmental and the autonomy of every system and tradition needs to be maintained. We could implement the following in our educational institutions to transcend to higher levels.

1. Every school should have a mandatory course that includes only the positive aspects of every major tradition, including atheism.

2. Almost everyone is born into a family that has a family tradition and faith. Call it a mother's tradition. Every student should choose one more tradition to learn, that perhaps could be the tradi-

on of one's neighbor. In India, neighbors are addressed as aunts and uncles by youngsters, so the student learns about the mother's and the aunt's faith.

3. Forced or coerced conversion should be made illegal. Historically, the invading armies of the West have inflicted terrible atrocities on local populations in the name of their religion. In the East, particularly in India, so-called protectors of knowledge and scriptures, due to their genetic selfishness, inflicted atrocities on their own people by dividing them based on the hereditary caste system.

Mahatma Gandhi in 1927 visited Sri Lanka and had no hesitation in declaring himself Buddhist. In his words, "Hinduism owes an eternal gratitude to that great teacher. He gave life to the teachings that were buried in the Vedas and which were overgrown with weeds. He made words in the Vedas yield a meaning to which the men of his generation were strangers." He suggested to the audience that Buddhists should learn about Hinduism and Hindus should learn about Buddhism. He then pleaded to look only on the positive and discard the negative aspect of each tradition. His message was the same about other traditions, including those of the West.

There are scholars who claim that Jesus survived crucifixion and died in his old age in India. Based on an article in the Hindustan Times (June 11, 2006), a team of German researchers and archaeologists is planning to visit Srinagar, India, to investigate the claim of a burial site of Jesus. There are books written on Jesus visiting India during his missing years (ages 12 to 30 of his life), and there are claims that he basically was a Buddhist. It is apparent that there is so much common to both traditions. Would it not be wonderful to discover that Christ was equivalent to Buddha incarnate? Humanity would certainly come closer to unification. Yes, there are differences in these traditions, but it is acceptable to have differences, as happens between siblings, as long as they are connected and not isolated.

Historically, Western traditions have been kept separated from Eastern traditions, thanks to Western imperialism cutting off the cultural roots of the West at the boundary of Greece and Turkey. Tom McEvilly writes in his book, *The Shape of Ancient Thought,* that Voltaire accepted that Indians were the first possessors of religious revelation. However, the British resisted the thought of attributing these roots to India, since India was their crown jewel and it would be difficult to rationalize their dominance over it.

Of Atom and Atman

Are the Atom and *Atman* worlds apart or closely related?

Two terms in Indian culture have fascinated me by a close similarity in their phonetics and the utter dissimilarity of their significance and essence. They are *Aham* and *Aum*, the first meaning "I-ness" and the second signifying the Ultimate Reality or *Brahman.*

We have already noted the two domains of the macro-world are the domain of goddess Lakshmi, who provides wealth and material well-being, and the domain of the goddess Saraswati, who provides education to acquire knowledge and wisdom. But what is the ultimate objective of individual life in all domains? The right objective and the right path, as the ancient masters would have put it, is to employ acquired wealth and wisdom to seek and achieve *Nirvana*, the end of all desires. When no desire is left, the self becomes selfless but with a feeling of love and unity.

In his book *Atom and Self,* Dr. D. S. Kothari said, "It is at least 2,000 years ago that the polarity of body-brain and mind, matter and spirit, energy and mass, outer life and inner life, the life of the senses and the life of the soul, the Atom and the *Atman* has been observed in India, since the *Upanishadic* period."

As another pair of opposites created by Nature, this polarity led to a dissociation of spiritualism and science, especially in European and

Western cultures. Over the centuries there has been a steady divergence between these two disciplines, until with the Newtonian revolution and the parallel Cartesian dichotomy in philosophy, it appeared that science and religion were at two extremes of human experience, one claiming to be rooted firmly in "material reality," and the other in "immaterial cognition."

With the pioneering work of Einstein, however, and the development of post-Einstein physics and quantum mechanics, the artificial dichotomy between the scientific and the spiritual quest, those two greatest of man's attempts toward the truth, began to collapse. Recall that *Time Magazine's* Man of the Millennium was Einstein and the runner-up was Mahatma Gandhi.

Dr. Kothari's book discusses masterfully, and from the point of view of an eminent scientist, how the polarities have been challenged and bridged by ancient Indian wisdom and by major, post-Einstein developments. Modern science has come much closer to the teachings of the ancient Indian sages.

A fascinating dialogue on the meaning of reality between Einstein and Rabindranath Tagore occurred when Tagore visited Europe to accept the Noble Prize in the 1930s. Einstein emphasized that science had to be independent of the existence of the observer, implying that the observations made by man are disconnected from the functioning of Nature. Tagore disagreed and maintained that, even if the Absolute Truth existed, it would be inaccessible to the human mind. Whatever we call Reality is revealed to us only through human faculties and human participation. The simple fact, expressed by Dr. Kothari, is that no observation or measurement is possible without a relevant theoretical and experimental framework, constructed by the total human self. Tagore was essentially stating the Anthropic Principle some 40 years before the British physicist Brandon Carter brought it into existence.

The relationship of the somatic and psychic selves and Nature needs to be understood in its many dimensions. While Western science can tell us much about this three-way relationship, many important, crucial dimensions, in which pathways to sub-ration, evolution, transcendence and harmony are to be found, have been explored by Eastern thinkers, ancient Indian sages of the *Upanishads*, and the six systems of knowledge that include Advaita Vedanta. Advaita presents the supreme achievement of monism through the processes of harmony. Forced monism is not monism; it has to come naturally in the realm of the psychological self. A jihadi or Taliban imposing monism by the sword offers only a mix-up of the somatic and psychic selves. It cannot work in the present-day world, and if imposed leads to slavery.

The philosophical self is at the extreme end of the psychic realm, at the border of the spiritual self, and exists in the natural world. However, Spirit, Soul, *Atman, Brahman* exist elsewhere. I recall a report of an investigation conducted in the 1940s in the popular journal, *Reader's Digest*. The story was narrated by my teacher, Mr. Vasani, and it tells of an experiment conducted by scientists where they put a dying man in a glass box, attached sophisticated instruments in and around his body to determine if the escaping soul, which they thought was in the realm of Nature and hence detectable by natural science, could be detected. No such luck—nothing was detected escaping the body when the man died. This is an example of materialists falling into a tangled hierarchy, explained by Amit Goswami in his book, *The Self-Aware Universe*.

How can an observer's consciousness observe the consciousness of a dying man? The consciousness common to all of us cannot be both observer and observed.

This is not to say that the somatic self is not important—quite the contrary. Enlightenment is possible through the human body. We do not know whether other creatures experience enlightenment. In the Buddhist scriptures, the Bodhisattvas were not confined to the human species. The bodily experience does not contradict spiritual experience. In fact, these experiences are associated with the law of evolution and the arrow of time. But a philosophic death is necessary to transcend from one domain to another. Sub-ration, stated differently, is a process of life where the tendency is to go from one level to the next without judgment, the prerequisite to transcendence.

There are many dimensions to man's being. The somatic and psychic selves are part of Nature, but *Atman* or Soul is not. Refinement is possible through training at each stage, but in jumps. These processes of refinement and sub-ration, evolution and transcendence continue for years. Man needs to move from animalist habits to human habits in all the different aspects of his life—eating, sleeping, interacting with others, and so on.

Thinking is a process that modern Western philosophy associates only with intellect. But the ancient Eastern tradition distinguished three types of thinking—associated with the intellect, the senses, and emotions. The first is logical thinking, conducted through the intellect of the mind. The second goes at times unnoticed but is of equal importance. It is behind all natural processes, within and without, microcosmic and macrocosmic, from the beat of the heart to the orbits of the planets and stars, and behind the complex but meticulous mechanism of the organs of the body, without which we cannot live. Intellect should never interfere with this process of thinking. The third is romantic, philosophic thinking, rooted in the emotions.

Hence, there is a great need to explore our connection with Nature, through the intellect but not confined by it, going beyond to use all the faculties available to us.

Chapter 5
Clustering, Harmony, Complementarities and Balance

Clustering and Unity within the Diversity of Four

Clustering is a natural tendency. A tribal man is lost when he is away from his tribe. The majority of people prefer to be part of a group. Grouping is universal. However, one does not need to be attached to groups, since in order to enter into the spiritual domain and merge with Universal Consciousness, there must be detachment from worldly matters

An analogy might be helpful. Driving on a four- or five-lane freeway in a place like California, one comes across clusters of cars, formed through speed limits. The "nature" of the freeway, its many lanes, speed limits, and so on, produces clusters "naturally," but the "enlightened" driver would stay out of such clusters to lower the probability of accidents with other cars. In the field of investment, it may be less profitable to be part of a herd. Often contrarians receive better returns on their investment.

I recall a game we played as children on weekends and holidays in the 1940s in India, before independence—the Non-Violent Resistance Movement (*Satyagraha*). Kids would get together in clusters, acting as freedom fighters. The objective for everyone was to get into a one-meter-square-sized area on the grass, called "the jail." The jail space would be a few feet away from about 25 kids who competed. Winners were those found in the square at the end of ten minutes. Smaller kids would not attempt to get into jail, since it was hard to compete with bigger and stronger kids. If I stayed with kids of my size, I could never get into jail. However, when I made an attempt, I succeeded in getting in the jail by finding a void, a little space for little me among the bigger kids. I was the happiest "contrarian" small kid to be part of a cluster of "giant" winners.

We all remember phrases like, "When it rains, it pours," or "Nature is always unpredictable, like fish swimming here and there with sudden twists and turns," or, more romantically, "Women are unpredictable, like autumn skies." What do such utterances really say beyond their surface meaning? I would suggest that these sayings indicate the significance and structure of clustering. Clustering is a non-uniform, uneven distribution of elements or events. It is a characteristic feature of Nature, as observed in the clustering of stars and planets. At the micro-level, the simple but lifesaving process of blood clotting in a wound is an instance of clustering. At the macro-level events occur in clusters, good or bad. Clustering is the cause of likes, dislikes, hate crimes, tribalism, empire building, and one of the Kennedy brothers in the Senate for over 50 years. If the clustering did not exist, the universe would fall apart. President George W. Bush became unpopular because so many unfortunate events occurred during his presidency though he was not responsible for most of them. These patterns occur also in the marketplace, in the movement of prices in the stock market, indicating the mass psychology of the stock traders. Clusters are therefore not only material but also psychic patterns. This gives more evidence that psychic selves are associated with Nature, like somatic selves.

Based on this, I will now introduce a special, basic pattern of clustering, namely unity but within the diversity of four.

There is already so much in the world that is divided into threes, starting with the basic division of many things as having a beginning, middle, and end. Certainly the Hindu Trinity of Brahma, Vishnu, and Shiva find some parallel in the Catholic Trinity of Father, Son, and Holy

Spirit. Jonah spent three days in the belly of a whale and Jesus spent three days in his tomb. One could also think of clusters of five—for example, there are five fingers, five basic elements, five gods in Hindu tradition, and five Ajivas in the Jain tradition. We could go on and on, but in our embracing three or five as a classic archetype, we have overlooked a more common occurrence of the number four. There are, after all, four seasons, four corners of the world, and four winds. If we look even closer, we can see that four, the number of stability, which can also be represented by two pairs of opposite or similar things, is perhaps the most common numeral in much of our daily life.

To begin our numerical study of the number four, we need to recognize that ancient Indians divided human existence into three autonomous domains, namely somatic, psychic, and spiritual. Western thinkers originally divided existence into three levels of Heaven, Hell, and Earth. The first two levels (somatic and psychic), associated with Nature, are also models for the number four, if we limit our focus to the natural part of our being that includes somatic and psychic levels and investigate their interrelationships and transcendence.

Firstly, Nature itself exists in multiple pairs of opposites. The four seasons of spring, summer, fall, and winter certainly form two pairs. Interestingly, these multiple pairs of opposites are also found within man himself. They are pairs that cannot be separated (for example, the north pole of a magnet cannot be separated from the South Pole). These two opposites, ancient Indians would say, need to "complement" each other instead of being at war, so that they can coexist in balance and harmony.

The recent application of the word "complimentarity" was introduced by the quantum physicist Niels Bohr. His observations were based on the discovery of subatomic particles such as electrons behaving as particles and waves (a pair of opposites). Bohr showed us that at the deepest levels of physical reality, things are not definitely spotty or smooth. This ambiguity is a result of neither vagueness nor contradiction, but Nature itself. An analogous situation can be described about a human person as a distinct individual or a nexus in the web of social interaction.

The implication of the principle of complimentarity is that a person is both an individual and a social component (another pair of opposites), and there is no need to separate the two. On a philosophical level, we can say that reality is "One" (Universal Self), and language is really its opposite, because it introduces unnecessary distinctions that need not be made. Bohr's strong belief in complimentarity led him to make a singular statement: "A great truth is a statement whose opposite is also a great truth." Recall comparing the truth with the beauty of a diamond or the story of the blind men of Hindustan and an elephant by the sages of India thousands of years ago.

Robert Oppenheimer, a physicist who led a team of scientists to develop the first nuclear bomb, tried to convince the world that the sciences and humanities are a pair of opposites; they complement each other and are not disconnected. He may have come to this conclusion based on his studies of Vedic scriptures in the original Sanskrit language.

Shankara in the eighth century stated: become a detached witness to learn about and understand nemesis. Even try to become "the other" in order to understand the opposite. Let us ask, what is this "opposite"? Pairs of opposites could coexist in balance and harmony if we learned to become detached witnesses, as preached by Shankara. Pairs of opposites could complement each other for a common cause. Take an example of a married couple. Husband and wife could compete and fight with each other, which could be destructive, or they could complement each other, maintaining balance and harmony with a result of better life for them and their children. There is another example from the field of children's education. Two global organizations—Pratham and Ekal—compete for donations but by complementing each other, bring in the most money for the poor children of India.

The number four, in modern times, is center stage through psychologist Carl Jung's work when he describes fundamental patterns of human thought not as *dyad* but *tetrad*, that is, two pairs of opposites having a to-tal of four elements in a balanced mandala-like arrangement, also known as "quaternary." Jung describes the quaternary as an archetype of almost universal occurrence. It forms the logical basis for any whole judgment; if one wishes to pass such a judgment, it must have this fourfold aspect. There are always four elements, four prime qualities, four castes, four ways of spiritual development, and four aspects of psychic orientation. The ideal of completeness is the circle of a sphere, but its natural minimal divi-sion is quaternary. Note that Jung talks about four castes and four ways of spiritual development, evidently influenced by Indian philosophy, which he may have discovered during his visit to India.

Jung describes the human body in four parts—sensation (body), feeling (emotion), thinking (intellect), and intuition (mind). His under-standing of intuition includes something other than or beyond sensa-tion, feeling and thinking. I interpret it to be associated with the initial condition of human existence, that is, genetics in the realm of human equipment. Perhaps I am taking a leap when I say that evolutionary change occurred during human history in four stages.

During the first stage, there was greater emphasis on the body and associated elements. The second stage was that of the mind. Then the in-tellect was emphasized. And the latest stage was the age of information and genetics. Based on our observation of life, it does not de-emphasize the fact that there are four stages to it, just as there are four elements (fire, air, water, earth) and four points on a compass (north, south, east, and west). Spiritually, recall that Buddhism had four Noble Truths and Christianity celebrates four Gospels that were actually mandated by a second-century book by St. Irenaeus, *Against the Heresies*, where the Eastern author pronounces the number four as being sanctioned by Na-ture itself in the four winds.

However, I would like to emphasize that Nature exists in multi-di-mensions, and within each pair of dimensions are two opposites. These pairs cannot be separated and each pair coexists with all the others. If we take this as a model of the total human self, we can conclude that one needs to learn to complement the opposites of oneself, and not be at war with oneself. By evolving and adapting to our changing environment, complementary pairs of opposites bring balance and harmony to our lives and help us to coexist with others. We can also realize that all four elements make up the whole with no one element being inferior or superior to the others, each one equal and coexistent, with its own autonomy and freedom.

A few additional examples are in order. Cluster formations are natural phenomena. Recall at the mega-level that stars form clusters in the cosmos; at the micro-level blood clotting happens in the human body; at the macro-level the old boys' club becomes the corporate world; Indians cluster in Little India; and so on. An organization, a form of a cluster, tends to become stagnant. If the CEO is not careful, it could stop evolving to higher levels or stop sub-rating. Organizations are almost always hierarchical. Leaders try to hold to their positions at the expense of the organization.

Detachment is more helpful to sub-rate, transcend, and move upward toward the mountaintop. Institutional hierarchies tend to generate empire builders and protectors who persecute those who do not fall in line. Living organisms exist in multidimensional space as multiple pairs of opposites. Organisms must find and exist at locations away from boundaries; they perish if they hit a boundary. It is necessary to maintain balance in a space with two pairs of opposites and four boundaries of quaternaries, as suggested by Jung and the ancient sages of India.

Tables 1 to 5 of different quaternaries and a *Summary of Tables* are given at the end of this chapter. The four elements of the total human self are connected to the four elements in different fields described by ancient Indian masters, mathematicians and physicists.

Note: Separations of opposites of each pair, in each category in the tables, are not unique, and cannot be exact. The process of separation and the identification of the four are debatable and changeable, as happens in Nature. Identification often becomes difficult when we do not know what we are trying to separate or when there are too many variables.

More on Multidimensional Space:

On matters of multi dimensional space constituted by pairs of opposites, deeper explanation is required. We exist in this space, but our existence is dynamic. It has to be—it cannot be stagnant, nature demands it. The characteristics of this space keep changing in time and we must adjust our position in this space to survive and prosper. These changes create fluctuations, like the movement of a pendulum but not necessarily at constant frequencies and amplitude. These movements are complex and mathematicians have tried to make these movements deterministic but with very limited success. Books have been written with titles like "Deterministic Chaos" etc. to prosper in various markets. No computers can solve such multidimensional problems accurately since the nature within and without is unpredictable.

However, humanity has learned a lot through experience and with the use of intellect and intuition. We have achieved limited success simplifying every problem. For example, talking about the movements of the pendulum, analogically we can find the frequencies, periods and displacement of these fluctuations. We would also know where and when the pendulum stops and changes its direction of movement. We also know that it spends the longest time at the location where it changes its direction and the least (minimum) time at the middle of the swing where the speed is the highest. Movements are necessary to be dynamic, to be alive. When we are talking about an organic life form, the heart has to keep beating, blood has to keep flowing. We are also dependent, for example, on the movements of the earth; it has to keep orbiting, but movements must be orderly, without hitting the boundaries of the space of our existence.

Guide to Tables 1 to 5

Tables 1 to 5 are self-explanatory by nature and structure. These tables lead us to observe fully a remarkable spectrum of the correspondence between the four aspects of Nature and the four domains of the total human self. Furthermore, there is also a correspondence between the four domains of the total human self and the four branches of mathematics; the four aspects of economics and political power; the four stages of life; the four systems of human motives; and several other sets of four.

In order to understand these tables, let us first note the categories that form their structure. They are: A: Nature; B: Total human self; C: Any specific field of their interaction, for example, mathematics or the four systems of human motives, and so on.

A: The four aspects of Nature are: Cosmic Order; Earth and Matter; *Avakasha* or Space, which is continuous and spacious; and Time, which is unidirectional, that is, thermodynamic and dynamic *(See Summary of Tables and Table 1, row 5)*.

B: The four domains of the total human self that interact with these four aspects of Nature are first, the DNA of the somatic self, which can be related to the origin—seeds (*Bijatma*), sperm or egg. The body of the somatic self (*Dehatma*) includes the heart, brain, and other parts of the body. The intuitive mind of the psychic self has the attributes of love (*Prematma*), devotion, belief, and the idealism of the philosophic self. The intellectual aspect of the psychic self has the attributes of reasoning, control, and other intellectual capabilities (*Gyanatma*) *(See Tables 1 to 5, row 1, and Summary of Tables)*.

C: The four branches of the foundational science of mathematics are: the theory of information, arithmetic, geometry, and algebra/calculus.

All items in the second column of all five tables are associated with genetics. We have seen how the theory of information with its dots corresponds to the genetic blueprint, with its seeds and drops. The information implies that there is stored potential energy in blueprints. They are also the initial conditions of order coming out of chaos that will progress in the future. The initial condition of investment is the initial capital to be invested in any enterprise. Information is also associated with the news media, the supplier of information, considered the fourth branch of the government. The initial creative idea goes a long way to provide a very high growth rate in any start-up enterprise.

Figure 5-1a Yin and Yang, a Pair of Opposites

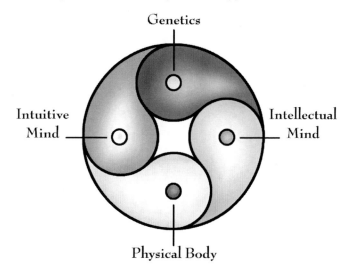

Figure 5-1b Two Pairs of Opposites

Items associated with the body of the somatic self are given in the third column of all five tables. The body is associated with discrete (digital) matter and organisms, and, considering its functions, actions and attributes, is associated with arithmetic, karma and karma yoga, matter, actions, gravity, employment, Karl Marx, the executive branch of government, and the earth. Autonomy, austerity, and being nonjudgmental are important attributes that the physical body should possess.

Items given in the fourth column of all five tables are associated with the intuitive mind of the psychic self, responsible for love, devotion, desires, intuition, spontaneity, spaciousness, and continuity. Geometry deals with specific shapes in space. It measures (metri) earth-spaces (geo). It can be seen that geometry is analogous to the space component of the intuitive mind. Shapes, real estate, and spaciousness are associated with geometry. Attributes of the intuitive mind include determination, compassion, desire, the act of willing, the path of subration, philosophic idealism, transcendence, and a devotional temperament, as discussed in Chapter 3. The legislative branch of the government prompts the executive branch to run the country's economy with an excessive money supply to maintain a lower unemployment rate.

Items in the fifth column of all five tables are associated with the intellectual mind of the psychic self. Algebra and calculus deal with certain aspects of temporality. They are analogous to the time components of the intellectual part (*Gyanatma*) of the psychic self. Intellect brings with it such evolutes as precise logic, logical reasoning, higher intellectual pursuits, as well as discipline and control of both body and mind. Conservative economists are concerned about the value of currency since they believe inflation is not good for people, certainly not retirees and those living on a fixed income. They control inflation by increasing the cost of money, that is, by increasing the interest rate. The function of the judiciary is to maintain law and order and adhere to the nation's constitution. Logical interpretation of the law becomes very important.

Referring further to the five tables, an example from the cult political history of mankind sheds further light on matters of clusters of four. Who could be a better example than Mahatma Gandhi? *(See Table 2)* He gave mankind a model of austere living and conducted the movement of *Satyagraha*, which has influenced the course of human history. From his autobiography and from many biographical-psychic studies on his life, it can be seen that his somatic self, especially his *Dehatma* or physical body, had unusually strong, good *Samskara*. The tough love he received from his mother Putalibai expressed itself in the three vows of external and internal cleanliness of the somatic self—to keep away from intoxicating drinks, meat-eating, and women—which his mother insisted on before permitting him to go to England to study law. Later, after fathering many children, he became celibate at the age of 40. His devotion to God, pure love for his country and the people of India, and his focused and controlled intellect is indicative of a strong, balanced psychic self.

Consider the matter of the somatic response to an impetus, a stimulus *(See Table 4)*. The response could be an over-reaction to a pluck of the string of a stringed instrument, like a guitar, sitar or violin. Or it could be a sluggish response due to a heavy lethargic body and/or mind. Neither of these responses is correct. The right response of the somatic self to any stimulus, physical or mental, is provided only by *Samskara*. It is important to note that the somatic self—genetics and the body—has to receive *Samskara* if the long and continuous process of sub-ration and evolution is to begin and continue.

An important instance of the correspondence of four is obtained in the ancient Indian organization of our life span into four divisions, presented as a temporal structure of life, with corresponding functions *(See Table 1)*. This function-based structure prompts, empowers, and ensures an orderly evolution of the individual self and of society. It is called *Chatur Ashrama Vyavastha*, The Order (*Vyavastha*) of Four (*Chatur*) Stabilities (*Ashrama*) of the lifespan.

These four stable periods of the lifespan are: *Brahmacharya ash-rama* (the stage of being a student and celibate, living away from home at a guru's school or *Guru-kula*); *Grahastha ashrama* (the stage of being a householder); the *Vanaprastha ashrama* (the stage of living in a forest home); and the *Samnyasa ashrama* (the stage of renunciation of all worldly ties).

A normal life span was expected to be 100 years and each stage was 25 years, the first one marked by an end of childhood *Samskara*, when a child passed through the rite of being "twice born," that is, being born again at the age of five as a *Brahmachari* or student (who literally "moves about in the *Brahman*").

Table 1 of Categories compares these four *ashramas* or stages of life with the four elements (genetics, physical body, intuitive mind, and intellectual mind) and with different kinds of interactions between the total human self and Nature.

Thus, *Brahmacharya ashrama* is an evolute of the second part of the somatic self, namely the body. It is the somatic self that receives *Samskara* and relates rightly to the *Brahmacharya ashrama*. The word "*Brahmacharya*" is sometimes taken to mean "celibacy;" it is only one aspect of *Brahmacharya*. This rich term derives from two Sanskrit words: *Brahma* and *Charya*. The former has a wide meaning, suggesting "Godhead" or "Ultimate Reality." The verb *Charya* means "to walk" or "to travel to." A *Brahmachari* travels toward what is Ultimately Real. This stage is marked by training the body and the pre-psychic self to obtain *Samskara*. What begins in this first stage, with the body, culminates in the final stage, with DNA.

The *Grahastha ashrama* is an evolute of the intuitive self within the psychic self. The word "*Grahastha*" derives from the word "*Griha*" which, in Sanskrit, means "home." *Grahastha* is a householder. This *ashrama* is characterized by the processes of experiencing and learning to play fair in the game of life. Its activities include the formation of family and acquiring wealth.

Vanprastha ashrama is an evolute of the intellectual self within the psychic self. The word *"Vanaprastha"* comes from two words—*Vana* and *Prastha*. The former means, in Sanskrit, "a forest" and the latter means "a city." This great language suggests, through juxtaposing what is ironically in most other cultures a reconciliation of wilderness and urbanity; of being outside a worldly ethos and of being in the world, being in society and out of society. In *Vanaprastha ashrama,* a person is free from desires for social gains, but is still involved in the well-being of the society. He does not expect or take anything from society, from the *Prastha*, yet he continues to contribute to society, in fact enhances his contribution and focuses exclusively on giving. What could be a better way of defining a proper place for seniors, for elders, for the grandfather generation, marked by a cultivated individual's nonprofit actions for the benefit of society? It is also associated with achieving recognition from society for these actions and for the state of such an individual's being.

Samnyasa ashrama is an evolute of the DNA part of the somatic self. The word *"Samnyasa"* derives from the word *"Nyasa"* and prefix *"Sam."* *"Nyasa"* means "put together" and *"Sam"* indicates propriety. *Samnyasa* would mean, in the Sanskrit so assiduously cultivated by ancient Indian sages, "Properly placed together." In the *Samnyasa* stage of life, the innermost, basic forces of life are put together properly. An inner pattern, a DNA design, is now organized in an orderly fashion. It comes from deep down, rooted in long life, perhaps life beyond birth and death, and is marked by austere living and the attempt to merge with Nature for the purpose of ascending to an afterlife.

Origin, Balance, and the Harmony of All

Let us look at the scientific units of measurement and units of the total human self, the former produced and used by the different branches of science, the latter I propose for use in the science or art of what I have called the *Samskaric* way of individual and global living.

We have learned about things of Nature through observation, experiences, intellectual thought processes, comparisons, and finally accurate measurements. There are fundamental units of measurement for length, weight, time, temperature, electrical energy, luminosity of light, and so on. We are familiar with such terms as meter and foot; gram and pound; second; ampere; Kelvin, and others. The rest of a unit's measurements are derived from the fundamental units of measurement in each branch of scientific observation. Different combinations of fundamental units provide us with more complex measurements. Thus, for example, velocity is measured in meters (a unit of length) per second (a unit of time); acceleration is determined quantitatively by measuring the change in velocity and is expressed in meters/second squared. Units of energy are obtained by multiplying force with distance or mass multiplied by acceleration multiplied by distance.

I propose taking somatic and psychic units as the basic units of the total human self, to be combined in different ways for our use. The optimum combination, I propose, would be the combination of four. We need to note that genetics and the physical body (from the somatic self) and intuition and intellect (from the psychic self) provide us with the four basic units of our total human self. The rest, which would include any field of human endeavor, can be connected to these primary units. This could be considered as a corollary to physicist Brandon Carter's Anthropic Principle, which states that the only things that can be known are those compatible with the existence of the knowers, the total human selves. From this could be derived the origin, balance and harmony of all.

The two groups in humanity, intellectuals and intuitivists need to be in balance and complement each other to bring harmony. The first group includes materialists and the second group includes religionists. As the population keeps increasing, the needs of the somatic selves keep increasing. It is apparent that the population of materialists keeps increasing. This trend needs to be checked and humanity needs to reverse it. Humanity needs more bridge builders to bring balance and harmony between intellectuals and intuitivists so that they complement and not compete.

The five tables represent the interconnectedness of everything to the total human self and Nature. They also describe the origin and evolutionary progress of humanity. I re-emphasize that the balance and harmony of the four in a particular field of human endeavor give us optimum results. After dividing the specific field of endeavor into four components, we must ensure that each one operates autonomously without interference.

One of the most successful examples appears to be the American government with their four autonomous components—executive, judiciary, legislative, and the national media, the information provider. It is remarkable that the government has endured assassinations, wars, Watergate, 9/11, and evolved to a level of complexity to minimize the effect of such events. It is not a perfect system of governance, but nothing in Nature is perfect. The most admirable part of the U.S. government appears to be that it is adaptive. In the words of Condoleeza Rice, the U.S. intends to follow the path that leads to "practical idealism." These same two words were uttered by the philosopher-kings of ancient times to uplift their subjects.

Another example is in the field of investment. Harry Markowitz received the Nobel Prize for proving that it is unsafe to put all your eggs in one basket. The implication is that one needs to invest in at least four non-correlating groups of investment to minimize risk. Four non-correlating investments associated with four elements of the total human self are growth stocks, treasuries and monies, real estate and resource stocks, and hard assets like portable gold coins and collectables, as shown in *Table 4*.

More on the Idea of Balancing the Four

We shall take the example of the current state of the economy (2008), where we are, and what we need to do to improve the situation. The four components in the field of economics, associated with genetics, the body, the intuitive mind, and intellect are: the GDP or economic growth rate, the unemployment rate, inflation rate, and interest rate, respectively. For a good economy, except GDP, all the remaining three components should be lower, possibly below three percent. Since America is a rich developed country, any number greater than three percent is desirable. Let us examine what the current situation is.

On August 21, 2008, I was fortunate to attend a one time movie event titled, "I.O.U.S.A." shown in 400 U.S. cities to give a critical message to the public. The movie was followed by a live panel discussion. Panel participants included Warren Buffett, CEO of AARP; Bill Novelli, Cato chairman of Niskanen; and David M. Walker, former head of Government Accounting Office (GAO) under both Clinton and Bush presidencies from 1998 to 2008. GAO is nonpartisan and keeps an eye on government spending and reports to Congress. The message from the movie and panel discussion was simple. America is heading toward a financial tsunami if we do not act immediately. We are all familiar with recent problems that include the sub-prime mortgage melt down, the housing bubble burst, nationalization of Fannie Mae and Freddie Mac, and bailing out the U.S. auto industries. The rising debt problem could accelerate toward the stratosphere. The problem is compounding due to almost zero household savings and uncontrolled consumption, and the rising cost of social security and medical benefits.

The debt could rise to over 50 trillion dollars in a couple of decades if no action is taken. If the projections are accurate, the most menacing culprit will be the rising cost of medical benefits due to the rising population of baby boomer retirees. Some of the proposed solutions were to increase the retirement age, change tax laws to increase the household savings, and better health management.

America has been on the wrong track ever since we let go of the production economy and went increasingly to a consumption economy. A ball park measure of production is the production of steel. The 19th century belonged to England because they were the largest producer of steel in the world. America was on the top in the 20th century because America was the largest producer of steel. The 21st century seems to belong to China since they are at the top in the same.

There has been a perception that we can maintain our standard of living just by innovation. If we use our minds, we do not have to produce steel or any other hardware in a factory. Some American economists would say about Asia and America that, "we think and they sweat." I would like to counter this by saying, "we must sweat, think, and philosophize" for our well being. There would be more people earning better wages in manufacturing than those employed in service industries if we were to adopt this course. Wealth is created by producing more, not by consuming more. We should never stop being creative and coming up with ideas that give us a better life. The rocket scientists, employed by the Wall Street, have done more damage to the financial markets; markets can not be controlled by employing only science. Rocket scientists are trained to solve the problems of technology and not the problems of the mind. We must go even further and enter the realm of psychology and philosophy. I believe economic laws have connections to savings, fairness, austerity, and many other human attributes.

More recently we have heard about peak oil, peak water, and peak food implying that these commodities will become scarcer in time because the production can not catch up with consumption. Yes, it is likely that it could happen since more people in Asia would like to have the same lifestyle as those in the West. Then there are two peaks that go hand in hand; they are peak consumption and peak stupidity.

Over consumption is not good for our health; obesity in the West is the highest. Why don't we have peak caution, not peak greed? I suppose greed caused the financial companies to be so highly leveraged. Now we are going in to the process of deleveraging. The pendulum is changing the direction from extreme greed and consumption toward caution and hopefully saving for a rainy day.

I hope, some time in the future America will lead the world to climb the mountain of austerity. Austerity here does not mean ascetic, but simpler living, avoid waste, live in a smaller house, drive a smaller car, and be environmentally friendly. Climbing a mountain is not an easy endeavor for anyone. America may have to descend a little, go around the obstacles as long as the direction is toward the mountain top. The day America is at the austerity mountain top will be a day to celebrate. We will be in harmony with nature around us, harmony of body, mind, and spirit.

Let us consider the period from October 1, 2008 through the first week of December 2008. The world is going through a financial tsunami and governments have not been able to establish market stability. Almost all markets have crashed, some slowly and some in a short period. The cause has been the implosion of money and credit, thanks to the investment made by banks in financial derivative instruments such as collateralized debt obligation (CDO), described by Warren Buffet once as "investment instruments of mass destruction". If one goes deeper to discover the cause of the current situation, it is the cheap money policy that created the technology and housing bubble along with the explosive rise in derivative instruments. It is amazing that no one among watch dogs saw the problem associated with wildly imprudent lending to anyone, credit worthy or not. It is pure lunacy to lend to totally unworthy applicants by assigning finite risk when we know that the risk is close to infinite. They did it by creating sub-prime (lower than prime) mortgages with variable interest rates. So how do we come out of this economic turmoil?

First, I hope they are able to bring reasonable stability in both financial and housing markets by injecting the liquidity and lowering the interest rate so that there is no collision with the boundaries of multidimensional space. Though I am a strong believer of free markets, the current situation needs government participation to protect the tax paying public. Government needs to take every possible step to keep unemployment under control, currently around six percent, keeping below 7.5 percent. As stated earlier, we need to focus on austerity and internal growth more so than the external. We need not increase the size of houses and automobiles that we use, but rather increase our *Samskara* to help ourselves and others in need. It is not desirable for an advanced economy to be dependent on imported energy. One way to reduce the dependence on petroleum is to adapt ourselves from the habit of driving big gas-consuming cars to smaller autos that would give close to 100 miles per gallon. It is true that wages are not on a par with productivity in Western countries, thanks to an abundant and cheap supply of labor in Asia. Another trend the world over, implemented by many governments, is not letting the economy fall into a deflationary cycle that could result in a depression that would create very high unemployment. Governments keep the cost of money low by keeping the interest rate low and injecting more money into the system. Maintaining a loose money policy helps governments manage large debt and employment.

In this economic environment, the losers are the creditors, retirees, and wage earners, and the winners are owners of hard assets and businesses with high growth. A large labor supply implies that there is a greater need for things requiring the mind and intellect in order to bring balance. Education, training, and *Samskara* help to balance each pair of opposites, and would enable wage earners to become more creative in competing to develop a demand for the products and services they provide.

Summary of Tables 1–5

Genetics	Physical body	Intuitive mind	Intellect
DNA, sperm	brain, heart	love, devotion	reasoning
Seeds, egg, origin	nerves, senses, reflexes	belief, intuition, spontaneity	logical, self-centered
Initial condition	digest, breath actions, walk	revelation, idealism	control, attention
News media radio talk	Executive branch	Legislative branch	Judiciary branch
Stored energy, information	earth, matter particles, organism, discrete	space, pacious, continuous, unlimited	time, dynamic flow, movement
Noise, chaos information order, initia condition	numbers, digits arithmetic, many quanta branches	analog, geometry, much, waves, fields, fractal	algebra, calculus, (non) linear, diff. equation, program
Stored action, *karma*, *Samskara*	action, *karma* yoga, austerity, training	devotion, *bhakti* yoga, love, compassion, fair play	knowledge, *gyana* yoga, attention, control
Initial capital invest, savings Adam Smith	goods/products services, Karl Marx	vendors/suppliers manufacturer, Maynard Keynes	consumer/users, demand, Friedman
Originator, Moses	proletariat, Karl Marx	love/Christ, Sigmund Freud	law giver, King David
Divinity spirituality imbedded in genes	existence autonomous nonjudgmental austerity	sub-ration, transcendence immanence compassion	harmony, complement control, balance

Table 5-1 Connecting the Total Human self with Nature, Ancient Philosophies, and Mathematics

	Somatic self		Psychic Self	
	Genetics	Physical Body	Mind	Intellect
Elements of the total human self	DNA, seeds, egg, sperm, origin	Includes brain, heart, senses, etc.	Love, devotion, belief, idealism	Logic, attention, control
From Vedic scriptures and ancient masters: the four stages of life	Sanyashrama: end-years of life merging with Nature for ascending afterlife	Brahmacharayashrama: training of somatic, pre-psychic, and psychic selves for better Samskara	Gruhastashrama: acquiring family and wealth, "fair-playing" the game of life; ascendance to the philosophical self	Vanprasthashrama: social work and achieving recognition; work without profit for charity
Four castes of ancient Indians	Kshatrias (protectors–soldiers), e.g., Rama, Krishna	Sudras (laborers, craftsmen, etc.)	Vaishyas (merchants, travelers)	Bramans (intellectuals, teachers)
Recommended functions for Moksha, release from bondage	Avoidance of re-birth with actions, devotions, and wisdom to the right	Karma yoga: path of action and austerity, convergence of a number of desires	Bhakti yoga: path of devotion, love and compassion, converging desires from many to "One"	Gyana yoga, path of knowledge, attention, and control over body and mind
Nature and the Cosmos	Energy (stored): origin, order, information	Matter: earth, oceans; a living organism	Space: Avakash	Time: dynamic flow (dynamic thoughts)
Jung's Quarternity	Genetics, DNA, seeds	Sensation (body, senses)	Feelings (love, devotion, intuition)	Thinking (logic, control)
Realm of math and physics	Information/Noise: zero, chaos, initial condition, order, genetics, blueprint	Arithmetic: numbers, digital, discrete particles; many	Geometry: blending, continuous, analog, fields, geometry of Nature; much	Algebra/Calculus: logical, programs, linear, nonlinear; differential equation
Religion: ignorance and wisdom of faith	Initiators, Christ/Buddha were not Christian/ Buddhist. "There are many paths to the mountaintop."	Persecutors, persecuted, empire builders, dogmatics: "My God is the only true god." Somatic greed.	Believers, philosophers (blind faith?): "Transcend from the rigidity of religion to the openness of spirituality."	Deconstructionists, self-centered or interconnected: "Religion is the opium of humanity."
Meditation: a state of being connected to the Universal Mind (Krishnamurti)	Samskara, a prerequisite for meditation	Non-existent self, brain without thoughts, images, memories; hardworking brain	Perception of explosion of love without a perceiver, silent, unchanging, infinitely conscious	Attention, control, without focus, center and directionless, disciplined, timeless intellect
Balancing pairs of opposites	Yin: energy, power, feminine	Yang: masculine, worker	Yung: Jung's human psychology	Yong: intellect

117

Table 5-2 Connecting the Total Human Self with Physics, Habits, and Other Forms of Human Endeavor

	Somatic Self		Psychic Self	
The four elements of the total human self	DNA, seeds, sperm (Bijatma), egg, stored energy and information	Body, brain, heart, digestive system, senses (Dehatma)	Intuitive Mind (Prematma), contemplation, spontaneity, revelation	Intellect (Gyanatma) logic, reasoning
Nature, environment, Cosmos	Blueprint order, stored energy, origin, chaos, initial condition	Earth, matter, particles, discrete, solid	Avakash, space, continuous spacious consciousness	Dynamic, awareness of time, movement of thoughts, flow/movement/air/water
Habits of successful wealth builders	Well-informed, endowed with good work habits, and Samskara	Work hard, karma yogi, enjoy working hard	Focused but flexible, movers, travelers, involved	Strong controllers of their habits of spending and saving; good winners and losers
Recommended functions	Ascend, transcend during and after life (to higher levels) with good karmas, follow dharma	Actions of giving, philanthropy for humanity and for other forms of life, an environmentalist	Determination, desires, willing, transcend with idealism to philosophic self, devotional, convergence of desire	Higher intellectual pursuits, discipline and control over body and intuitive mind
Example using M. Gandhi	Became celibate after age 40	Austere living and movement of Satyagraha	Helping others with love and devotion	Controlled experiment in truth
Rudy Rucker's math tools	Information tends towards infinity and is irreducibly complex.	World can be expressed/resolved into digital bits	These bits form a fractal pattern in fact/true space	Godel's incompleteness theory, i.e., patterns are indescribable and incomplete logically
The four forces of Nature	Weak nuclear force (Bosons), sub-atomic distances	Gravitational force (Graviton), (astronomical scale), proportional to masses (body mass)	Electromagnetic force (Electron photon), establishes continuous field (Sheldrake's morphic field),	Strong nuclear force (intellect is considered most desirable component of man), particles are Gluons
Complimentarity of Prigogine and Kothari, description: time domain, activities and processes	Micro-matter, DNA, atomic and subatomic dynamic particles, undistinguishable; reversible processes; mysterious quantum jumps; noncontinuous; act of detection will disturb the outcome	Macro-matter, live system, organism, organs, nerves, body, distinguishable; irreversible processes of decay; body can be observed, operated on and "repaired," and cured	Feelings, pain, pleasure, goal, purpose, chooser, involved, participant, unique; irreversible (thermodynamic); difficult for an observer to be observed	Brain, stored memories, why and why not; recallable thoughts; dynamic; one can go back in time to bring back from old memory. Thoughts jump from one to the next like a quantum jump and are indivisible. The act of observation of the thought process will disturb the outcome.

Newtonian mechanics	Energy E=Fx (X2-X1) Power P=VxF	Mass M, moving from distance X1 to X2	Velocity V and acceleration A	External/ Internal resisting force F F=mass M x acceleration A
Electrical science	Power P=E/T=EI=I2R	Electric charge Q; I=Q/T	Current I=Q/T T=time	Electromotive force=V= voltage; Resisting force=IR; R=resistance
Economics of goods/services	Stored wealth; capital; investments; savings are seeds of wealth	Needs of goods and services	Supplied by venders and manufacturers	Demand=Applied force; Price=Resisting force
Responsible economist (MIT dictionary)	Adam Smith: strong economic foundation, wealth of nations	Karl Marx: focus on proletariat	Maynard Keynes: inflationary economy; elastic money	Reagonomics; Milton Friedman: supply side economy

Table 5-3 Connecting the Total Human Self with Economics and other Fields of Human Endeavor

System	Somatic Self		Psychic Self	
Elements of the total human self	Genetics (DNA, egg, seeds, sperm)	Body (heart, brain, hands, legs)	Intuitive mind	Intellect
Self, math, and Nature	Information, order, origin, energy	Number, digits, discrete, arithmetic, matter, action	Continuous, blending, geometry, love, space, expansion	Dynamic, algebra, calculus, time, differential equation
Economy and measures of economy	Creativity, growth rate of GDP	Rate of (un)employment	Inflation rate; consumer, and producer price index	Cost or money, interest rate
Symptoms of inflation	Real growth may be low or (–ve)	Though low unemployment higher taxes due to higher prices, high tax	Too much money chasing fewer goods and services, high CPI** and PPI*, (inflation rising)	With loose and cheap money economy out of balance; productivity declining
Good, balanced economy	True growth and increasing creativity and productivity	Low unemployment, trained workers with good work ethics	Growth of money due to high productivity, low CPI** and PPI*	Optimum use of capital/resources and low interest rates
Centrist government and biases of elements	*Laissez-faire*: libertarian, minimum government, high production	*Authoritarian*: less liberties, high taxes, currency control, nationalization, loss of liberty	*Socialism*: left, liberal bias to take care of all; excessive, inflationary money growth	*Conservatism*: rightist, higher cost of money and capital, high interest rates
Bias toward each category and potential problems	*Laissez-faire* safety net of government may not exist, criminal activities could accelerate due to small government	Could bring revolt due to too much authority — at the mercy of authority — could create high unemployment — corruption, poverty, cheap labor	High inflation, high taxes, poor growth, wasted resources, suppressed creativity — "bubble" economies, loss of motivation and creativity	High cost of money/capital; also could suppress growth and could create credit crunch — more bankruptcies and foreclosures, deflation, wages lagging behind productivity
Solution to the potential problem	Education/training for balanced growth, directed toward internal growth	Education (training for good work ethics), harmony, democracy, austerity — good for environment	Controlled money growth and population growth, smaller families, encourage more entrepreneurship	High excessive interest rate is a form of taxation — should be moderate — more capital should be available for growth
Associated investments for better returns	Growth and value, stocks, high yield bonds, businesses, growth/peace investments, savings	Gold bullion, rare coins, collectable; for privacy and portability, crises investments during Nazism, communism	Real estate, resource stocks, collectables, inflation hedges, war investments	Bonds, treasuries, bank, financial stocks, high yield stocks, investment in deflationary economy

Avoiding investments when there are:	Cash, gold, precious metals, diamonds in a lawless anarchy	Stocks, bonds, real estate and the government is criminal and corrupt	Long-term bonds, life insurance and annuities, treasuries, cash in a hyperinflation environment	Stocks with no yield, no growth and little value and commodities in a very highinterest environment
Branches of government	*National media*: information provider (4th branch)	*Executive branch*: "economy stupid,""employment stupid"	*Legislative branch*: pork barrel spending, "inflationary" legislation	*Judiciary*: intellectual-logical, law and equal justice
Four systems of human motives; UCLA Prof. Fiske	*Communal sharing*: equality, equivalent, undistinguishable; like atomic particles	*Equity matching*: primitive; barter like carpools; no legal tender involved	*Authority ranking*: hierarchy in organizations; transcendence; desire to move to higher level	*Market pricing*: logical; pricing is resistive to the flow of goods and services

*PPI = Producer Price Index

**CPI = Consumer Price Index; currency of economy = money; currency of politics = political power

Table 5-4 Connecting the Total Human Self with Miscellaneous Field of Human Endeavor

	Somatic Self		Psychic Self	
Four elements of the total human self	DNA, genetics, (potential stored information), egg, sperm, origin	Body, heart, brain, particles, digital, statistical	Intuitive mind	Intellect (upper/lower)
Stock investment, attributes	Information/wisdom (diversification) to reduce the risk; the wisdom of experienced investors is better than the successful but young adviser.	Digital statistical, technical analysis; to buy and sell, re-move emotions; gap/quantum jumps in up and down price	Emotions of greed and fear; patience is a better virtue than intellect; mass psychology determines the direction of markets	Fundamental valuation; different ratios (PE, PS, PEG*) growth, data, yield interest rates determines value; buy "business" that is easy to understand
Real estate attributes	Wisdom: governmentsponsored tax advantages; media advertisements	Maintain lower vacancy and lower management cost to be successful	Space, location, location good investment during inflation	With low interest rate, high leverage, take advantage of OPEOM*
Response of the total human self	*Samskara* may influence the response	Excessive *Kafa* (heavier body), and sluggish, slow *Under-reaction*	Excessive *Vatta* (lighter) but mentally unstable *Over-reaction*	*Pitta* and balanced, good intellectual control *Right response*
Guy Murchie's *Seven Mysteries of Life*	1) Abstraction; an egg sperm separate, but originate from another body, packed info in seeds, i.e., packed energy 2) Germination, begin growing 3) Divinity and spirituality in genes EGG; DNA	4) Earth is a super somatic body within, and "onion-like" 5) Cells in bodies, organisms on earth, earth within cosmos; we are all at least 50th cousins to all others; existence autonomous ONION	6) Transcendence, a bridge – mind/psyche is a bridge from somatic to the gate of spirituality; symbiotic existence but with a link, a bridge to transcend from finite to infinity, open space of spirituality TRANSCENDENCE, BRIDGE	7) Polarity, two opposites, man and woman and many more pairs, recognized by intellect; balance maintained and controlled by intellect; complementarity and harmony of opposites BALANCE

Six security threats categorized by the United Nations dated December 2004	1) Ethnic/genetic interstate rivalry or "junction" wars, e.g., India/Pakistan, African tribal rivalries	2) Human Body, problems, starvation, poverty, diseases 3) Civil War, collapsed/failed nations;	4) Jihadism, terrorism due to "brain washing" 5) Trans-national, organized, drug related crimes	6) Threat of mass killings due to intellectual weapons, (WMDs*) nuclear and biological
Historical sages and scholars	Moses: Originator, attention to the Creator, focus to the skies. Buddha	Karl Marx: attention to the proletariat; Gandhi	Sigmund Freud; Carl Jung: focus to the mind and subconscious	King David: the law giver; focus to the intellect; scientists

Abbreviation Guides: PE: Price to Earning Ratio; PS: Price to Sales Ratio; PEG: Price to Growth Rate; WMDs: Weapons of Mass Destruction; OPEOM: Other People's Money

Table 5-5 Connecting the Total Human Self with Economics, Politics, and Other Fields of Human Endeavor

The four elements of the total human self	DNA	Body	Mind	Intellect
Art of organizational strategy, *Alexander The Great* by Partha Bose	Lacking succession contingency; plans contradictory to genetics; multitude of sperms to have higher probability of conception	Strong leader, empire-builder implies weaker successors; promoting loyalty over talent	Suppressing criticism leads to conformity, obedience and blind faith; associates avoid rocking the boat no matter what	Strong leader's success is based on fundamental value judgment and public actions, more focused on integrating and unifying known world; no interest in institution building
Attributes of money/currency	*Storable* (Like stored wealth, stored information) children are "capital"; grandchildren are like "interest rate"	*Discrete* Countable transportable, recognizable, having standards like coins (gold/silver rather than paper)	*Convertible* Transferable, exchangeable for other goods/services, need faith in the issues (government, corporations)	*Controllable* Enforcing waste, for pleasure, frivolous, sentimental; changeable in value based on interest rate must be secure
Federal reserve and its functions	Functions to stimulate or retard national economy to achieve balance	Adjust change in reserve required among member banks	Buying, selling government bonds changes, flow of money both ways, positive and negative	Changing and controlling interest rate among member bank
Henry Kaufman's model	*Marketability*	*Money*	*Liquidity*	*Credit*
Indian leaders and their contribution	Informers and initiators of independence (Tilak, Gokhale, Gandhi)	Gandhi, karma yogi, *Satyagraha*; Patel, Bose, the integrators of India as a nation	Gandhi, the lover of humanity; Tagore, the poet; Vivekananda	Vivekananda, Aurobindo, Tagore, Radhakrishna; intellects of Indian thought

Chapter 6

Bridge Builders and Coexistence

Builders of Bridges

Some words need to be clearly defined before using them in the course of serious inquiry, for example, "bridge builder." Who is a bridge builder, and what is a bridge? A bridge is a path connecting two land masses separated by water. When we refer to bridges between two different cultures, say India and America, which seem to be diametrically opposite, what do we mean?

We are referring to the cultural, religious, social, and other connections between these two nations. These subtle "bridges" between India and the West have come in a variety of forms from various individuals in their histories—whether it was Dr. Martin Luther King introducing Mahatma Gandhi's *ahimsa* as a cornerstone to his civil rights movement in America, or the music maestro Pandit Ravi Shankar making *"sitar"* a household word among music lovers in America.

Among the first bridge builders in the first decade of the 20th century was Swami Vivekananda, who participated in a conference of world religions and held the audience spellbound. His influence indirectly affected the writer Frank Baum who wrote several books, including the American classic *The Wizard of Oz*. Writer Ardeep Dhaliwal claims that there is some influence of Indian scriptures in Baum's work. Another early bridge builder was J. Krishnamurti, who was raised and educated by the Theosophical Society, co-founded by Annie Besant, who was an activist and a supporter of Irish and Indian self rule.

Late in the year 2004, former President Clinton, at the opening of the Clinton Library, declared that he planned to spend the rest of his life bridge building. I believe every one of us should spend more of our lives bridging the gaps between people of different views and cultures. Every Indian tradition accepts the view that human existence lies within the multiple boundaries of two opposites, discussed in the previous chapter. Indian tradition also believes in balancing the opposites in harmony, while complementing each other.

Building bridges allows us to establish contact, communicate, and synthesize differences. In this wider and subtler sense, bridge building between India and America has expanded dramatically to include economics, trade, entertainment, media, medicine, defense and science. In fact, we are witnessing an exciting communication explosion, thanks to the high-speed connectivity of the Internet. Any given network is represented by links (line, bridges) and nodes (centers, circles). Our tendency is to give greater importance to centers more than links. I believe we need to give equal importance to links, that is, bridges and their builders.

I wrote an article entitled "The Bridge Builders" (*India Post*, 2004) about bridge builders whose last names, it so happens, rhyme. These are Dr. Ravi Batra, Dr. Fritjof Capra, and Dr. Romesh Japra.

In earlier chapters I wrote about *Samskara* and the three dimensions of the total human self. They are the somatic or pre-psychic self and its evolutes, the physical body and genetics; the psychic self and its evolutes, the intuitive and intellectual mind; and the spiritual self, quite different from the first and second dimensions because it is associated with the human soul. And there is a fourth dimension external to the human body—the environment or Nature.

I repeat this, albeit "in a nutshell," because it is in this important area of interaction between man and Nature that I perceive a deeper relation among the bridge builders. There is greater significant rhythm in their understanding of the interaction between man and Nature in the fields of economics and ecology and the third dimension of human personality, namely the spiritual self.

Dr. Batra, a professor of economics, has been able to connect the fourth dimension of the human personality, namely the economic activities involving the interaction between man and Nature, to the third dimension of the human personality, namely human spirituality. He came to prominence when his 12th book, *The Depressions of the Nineties*, was first published. A large number of future trends and events in economics that he predicted in the book proved to be accurate. His more recent books, *Greenspan's Fraud* and *The New Golden Age,* are even more relevant today than books published before. This earned him much respect from lay readers as well as from specialists in economics. The accuracy and dependability of his observations and predictions stemmed from his ability to integrate spiritual truth with economic observations.

Dr. Fritjof Capra is an eminent professor of physics. His contribution to human knowledge has earned him worldwide respect. In his best-selling book, *The Tao of Physics*, he made a connection between the intellectual mind and a corresponding spirituality by employing Eastern scriptures for the task.

Dr. Japra is a respected cardiologist and founder of the journal *India Post*. His contribution comes from the relationships he established between the somatic self and Eastern spirituality through a different pathway, that of spirituality through action or karma yoga. His widely read newspaper provides a national forum of ideas and information shared by its large number of readers.

These bridge builders have made significant connections in their own unique ways to the third dimension of the human personality—human spirituality. They have demonstrated how the Eastern scriptures, especially the philosophies of Buddha and the teachings of the wise sages of ancient India, can be integrated into the dynamics of Western life.

That focus on integration is a bridge that we all need to cross. The world needs more bridge builders whose rare, clear vision inspires us all.

The Truth of Harmony

A focus on harmony and integration enables and compels us to look closely at the processes and forces that make such a state possible. The more we focus, the more aware we become of the difficult task before us.

India's renowned scientist and former president, Dr. Abdul Kalam, said in one of his earliest speeches that we need to transcend from religion to spirituality. What is "spirituality"? Philosophically, spirituality implies idealism and when associated with religion, it alludes to religious existentialism. Religion seems rigid and confined within set boundaries, while spirituality seems open and in an infinite space of consciousness.

Dr. Kalam's comments appear at first glance to reflect a joyful concept, an oasis of noble desire within a desert of harsh reality. They seem to represent a reaching out for a higher certainty from within a world that claws and scratches at things it cannot hold onto. As one looks around our unstable globe, one sees many armed camps hostile to one another. There are ceaseless fights for territory and resources. Religions try to impress the correctness of their own view of God and of "the truth."

However, Dr. Kalam's comments, though brief, are profound and link up with what Mahatma Gandhi lived by and died for. Gandhi identified and lived for *sarva dharma samabhava*—equal respect for all paths. Gandhi was one of the strongest proponents of *sarva dharma samabhava* because he was a keen student of many different religions. As man is fallible, imperfect and flawed, he cannot be sure what "truth" is; he therefore has to be open-minded and soul-searching.

Gandhi's attitude of and insistence on equality in the acceptance of all religions was rooted in his belief that God is Truth, and later that Truth is God. The statement implies that the concept of truth, one of the attributes of God, occurred in the human mind before the concept of God. Professor Parekh, in his book *Gandhi*, explains that Gandhi thought of this statement because it seems to be more inclusive; it would also include atheist truth-seekers. Gandhi was also guided by the Jain theory of many paths, which compares truth not to a feature-less monolith but to a diamond with many facets. Each facet looks as beautiful as any other, as we rotate it and view it from different angles. The truth of nature can be deceiving; the answer is the acceptance of many facets of truth due to Heisenberg's uncertainty principle and many quantum possibilities. Each religious tradition, similarly, should be seen and appreciated for its own approach to God, without judging any one approach as superior or inferior to any other.

We have looked at the story of the blind men touching different parts of an elephant's body, each man concluding that the shape of the whole elephant was like the shape of the particular part he had touched. So, too, the various religious traditions create a multitude of concepts, visions and images of God.

India is a country that historically has welcomed all faiths—Jewish, Buddhist, Sikh, Christian, Muslim, Jain and Hindu—with an understanding that all these rivers merge into the ocean of God. The Indian constitution that Gandhi, Patel and Nehru helped to form emphasizes a secular respect for each religious tradition, and India, we hope, will never lose that spirit. More than five decades ago, Prime Minister Jawaharlal Nehru proposed the political philosophy of the peaceful coexistence of nations through his vision of *pancha sheela*, the five-fold correctness of international relationships. This involved the notion of "live and let live," rather than an insistence that the other should change in order to join company. Different traditions and cultures have coexisted side by side in India for centuries.

There are two options before us: "melting pot" or "patchwork." The former insists on the giving up of one's identity before joining in. The latter permits a peaceful coexistence based on rules of harmony, *pancha sheela.*

When Steven Deon, Canada's minister of information, said, "India's patchwork of coexistence may help the world learn how to coexist," he was not only acknowledging the cultural changes taking place in his own country, but he was also reminding us of India's rich history of philosophy extending back thousands of years. A range of visionaries—from Buddha, Mahavira and the Vedic seers; through emperors like Janaka and Ashoka; builders of systems of philosophy like Kapila, Kanada, Shankara, Madhva and Ramanuja; to modern sages like Tagore, Aurobindo, Gandhi and S. Radhakrishnan—opens before our eyes. This reveals an impressive assemblage of men who recognized India's cultural tapestry and pointed out that introspection and accommodation are far better means for the advancement of humanity than brute force and material conquests.

Sri Aurobindo, for example, believed that we should seek God through involution—inward evolution, achieved through introspection, in which we reach out for the Divine and the Divine reaches out for us. Through Sri Aurobindo's involution, one learns to move away from *Aham* (self-centeredness, arrogance and hatred) and move toward *Aum* (Universal Love).

Philosopher and former president Radhakrishnan pointed out that intuition, as a faculty of the mind, is more useful than intellect in order to know Reality and Godhood. One's true self, Soul, and God or the Absolute Supreme Being are like the light of a candle and the light of the sun. A prism would separate the same seven components of light (ROY G BIV—red, orange, yellow, green, indigo, and violet) in either case; the only difference between the light of the candle and of the sun is in intensity. The analogy implies that man is, in essence, Divine, and also that every man is equally of divine essence.

The great Indian poet, Rabindranath Tagore, proclaimed that re gion is needed to establish unity in diversity, but religion can only be effective when it has spirituality at its core. For Tagore, the substance of spirituality was Universal Love. Love does two things: it binds humanity together but it also extends the reaches of humanity outward to include much more. Ultimately, love binds all living creatures together. Tagore's philosophy envisioned a true evolution that aimed at removing hatred and instead loving mankind and all life.

The philosopher poets and saints, both men and women, continue to send nourishing streams of wisdom and to provide protective shields against devastating windstorms of non-*Samskaric* forces. Mirabai, the great Indian poet from the 16th century and a profound saint, renounced her princely family, royal wealth and position, and risked her life for her austere and complete devotion to Krishna and inspired, some four centuries later, another great Indian, Mahatma Gandhi. He has compared Mirabai to Socrates.

Mirabai too was asked to drink poison by the ruler of her native state because, like Socrates, she held views and convictions not acceptable to the powers of that time. When asked, in the year 1947, the year of India's independence from the British Empire, whom he would like to see as the president of India, Gandhi replied that he would like a young girl from the lowest caste of India, an untouchable, as the first president of free India, challenging the British who had crowned Queen Elizabeth when she was just 17.

Likewise, another woman of "pure heart" from Indian history was Catherina, whose extraordinary life has been described by the Mexican poet and Nobel laureate, Octavio Paz. In his book *Lights of India*, Paz traced the career of this great woman. She was a princess born in a royal family in western India and was a devotee of Krishna. Abducted by pirates, she was taken to the Philippines and then sold to a *Samskaric*, elderly, noble Mexican couple who took her to Mexico. In the course of her painful but courageous journeys in captivity, her devotion to Krishna was transformed to an equally deep devotion to Christ. Sainthood was bestowed on Catherina by the Mexicans. Like Mirabai, Catherina knew how to transform her pain and humiliation into love of God. Like Mirabai, she found profound freedom through austerity, spiritual love, and introspection. We are reminded by Mirabai and Catherina that there are many pathways to the mountaintop.

Kabir, another great Indian poet and a Sufi saint, from the same period as Mirabai, taught the same message of tolerance and understanding of different religions, and was a source of nourishment for Tagore and Gandhi. Kabir has written a lovely poem on the self-sacrifice required of all who dare walk the path of spirituality.

"As the wood-cutter advanced, the trees sighed and said: 'It matters nothing that we are to be cut down. But alas, the birds will lose their homes.'" Kabir also wrote, "You will die one day, perhaps tomorrow; Grass will grow on your tomb; Your friends will forget you. Therefore, try hard in knowing your soul." When I die, I leave my wealth where ever it is, at home and few other places. My family and friends go with my dead body to the cemetery where the body is either burnt or buried, and then they go home. The only thing left are my good selfless deeds that people will always remember.

At the start of a new millennium, we watch armies move into foreign lands as they have for thousands of years, and terrorists violate boundaries within and without. We see all this and wonder if the kings, presidents, and religious leaders of today's world appreciate the value of introspection and patchwork coexistence, allowing all to live in their own way.

Christ was not Christian; Mohammed was not Muslim; Buddha was not Buddhist, and Ram was not Hindu. The teaching of all four "visionaries" tells us that anyone can become a Christ or a Mohammed, a Buddha or a God. Empire and cult builders have appropriated and polluted our great spiritual legacies for thousands of years. Let us wish, with President Abdul Kalam, that people from different places can transcend by employing different religions to reach a higher state of being.

From Paradigm to Process

We have just examined contemporary bridge builders and historical makers of harmony, seen as models and paradigms in our search for harmony and transcendence. Now our attention shifts from paradigms to the processes toward that purpose.

Tools used by mankind to study cultural evolution include computer software (language and mathematics) and hardware (the telephone, computer, automobile, and house). Cultural evolution also depends on choices made by humanity. How does man act? Actions are taken based on desired goals and values. In this context, it is important to note that there are "feedback loops" to control the outcome in the process. Though there is "freedom to choose," actions are controlled by feedback loops, bringing praise, blame, rewards and punishments. There are cherished values, ethical and legal codes, guilt and gratitude. The great thinker Henry Bergson believed that freedom in its purest form manifests itself in creative acts. I believe that creativity will increase with the degree of *Samskara*.

Subjective experiences of freedom and a blissful mind are due to creative processes. Eastern order-creating processes like yoga, vipassana, acupuncture, and ayurveda are very old, and are now being adopted by the West. These processes need to be explored more.

The future is open. Truth is natural and personal and is knowable through both reason and experience. Experience and reason convey truth more than authority. Truth is revealed occasionally through spontaneous "revelation." Knowledge of objective truth can never be final and complete. There is no such thing as an Absolute in Nature, including in the somatic and psychic domains. However, truth obtained from personal experience may not be communicable and it is certainly not transferable. The ultimate human goal is unity of everything: unity of fundamental sciences, unity of natural forces, and unity of humanity. This brings us back to the perception of two evolutions—external and internal—through which these three unities can be attempted and achieved.

Pairs of opposites will always exist. They are two sides of the same coin. In the origin of sciences, there has been a reductionist approach based on division and objective analysis. How can that approach unify? There is the state of being, and there is the process of becoming. Being an objective observer separated from the rest of the world results in an outcome of reductionism. Becoming, that is, participating and experiencing integration, on the other hand, seems to be the way toward unification.

Unification needs a careful and creative approach. It appears to be quite simple. The approach to unification should itself be based on unification—it cannot be based on reductionism. It should accept the whole, both sides, both opposites, both the so-called good and the so-called bad. Recall that bad is not bad, it is only ignorance. Indian scriptures state without hesitation that bad is the raw material for good. Unification may be possible through the experience of becoming selfless, losing identity and becoming united with Nature.

Based on this, I believe there is an urgent need to develop and progress along with science. It should be developed through fields that include psychology, sociology, philosophy, and economics. Revolutions, riots, and market crashes are in many ways chaotic. There is a need for better control to minimize the effect of such events. For this, it is necessary to employ both reductionist and integrative approaches, and both Western and Eastern approaches could accelerate order in these non-scientific fields.

Before we conclude this discussion on the processes of order and evolution, let me add a brief note on three terms—evolution, growth, and expansion. Humanity has been learning about the external world or Nature for millennia. We are familiar with phrases like "westward growth and expansion" in the history of the USA; of galactic expansion in astronomy; of population growth and expansion; economic growth; and the conquering and controlling of Nature. There is an old Chinese proverb that in essence states that, grow grain for one year—prosperity; grow trees for 10 years—prosperity; and grow people for 100 years—prosperity. We have done well in growing the world population. However humanity lags behind in inner growth, inner expansion, learning more about ourselves, and controlling our somatic and psychic selves. Implementing *Samskaric* training on a larger scale would be the first step in the right direction.

The World Is a Patchwork of Coexistence

Patchwork coexistence is essentially the same as the principle of *pancha sheela* coined by Prime Minister Nehru, one of the founders of the "non-aligned" movement that in and of itself was a patchwork of nations. One of the important principles of *pancha sheela* was to have nations coexist with autonomy without any interference from other nations. Whether it is the vast Roman Empire and its diverse cultures that extended from Britain to Persia and North Africa, or India with its own remarkable diversity of dialects, religions and peoples, one sees commerce, communication, and trade flowing between people of different backgrounds when given the chance. Humans, after all, exist at two different levels, both as individuals and also in communes, like sub-atomic particles (as particles and waves). Though we suffer from prejudices and xenophobia, we can find common ground to coexist. America, a land of diverse cultures, is trying to adapt to this phenomenon.

However, when two cultures interact, stereotypes often emerge as a way for people to identify others who are different. With these stereotypes often come resentments, fear, and even aggression. Wars can result from this division of community, and self-perpetuating violence may be a legacy for generations to come. A brief look at Palestine today, or in Iraq and Iran between Sunnis and Shias, shows some of the fallout of unsuccessful patchwork coexistence. But the negative effects of cultures rubbing against each other has equally found its antidote when a younger more idealistic generation crosses the cultural barrier and cultivates marriages that can bridge centuries of mistrust, confusion, and war. Some sociologists have suggested one of the ways to resolve issues of historical animosity is by bringing youth together from two feuding groups and getting them married. With this "Romeo and Juliet" bonding, future generations tend to overlook and forget historical feuds and instead look only for the best and what is positive in the two cultures.

In reference to the three selves discussed previously, they are in reality multiple sub-layers like an onion, with each previous self being the mother of the next. The ancient Indian Vedic teachers knew that unless somatic needs are first met, it is extremely difficult to move on to the next level. Ancient sages knew that to mix these selves by regression was very dangerous. Autonomy at every level, sub-ration and transcendence were strongly recommended. When cultures freely mix without accepting and reverencing their own uniqueness, the pot of soup can become a swirling caldron of confusion.

People choose their layer of existence based on the equipment they possess. The Eastern teachings often saw this training translated into a game of life where the objective was to sub-rate and transcend within one's own self. To transcend is to put effort toward this goal.

Our existence is dynamic. In almost any society, certainly in the USA and India, I have observed almost everyone at the same level of existence working for their somatic needs. Their activities of choice are in a layer most appropriate to their natural equipment. Moreover, physical needs have to be taken care of before one can transcend to higher levels. This process of fulfilling somatic needs apparently finds itself most suited to the American system because of the basic American philosophy of freedom of the individual. The state of the American social system based on human values is not perfect but probably one of the best.

Problems can arise between cultures and peoples with the mixing of beliefs and basic wants manifested by interaction. These problems can parallel the mixing of the different selves due to regression. However, people of different "layers" in cultures can and do coexist side by side, even in one family. It is the interaction and activities that should not be mixed. The somatic and psychic selves are, though connected, separate domains each having its own space and boundaries. To transcend from the somatic to the psychic space, one needs to cross the boundary, implying the philosophic death of the somatic self to be reborn as the psychic self.

The prerequisites to transcend, in order, are: autonomy, detachment, and sub-ration. By encouraging sub-ration, members do not feud over their paths; rather they find themselves journeying together to a mountaintop of transcendence. This journey may be by their unique paths, but the participants are still together in the process.

One of the benefits of transcendence is that as one moves from the somatic to the psychic level, somatic needs lessen and keep decreasing as one approaches the spiritual self. We often idealize that in God's realm there are no pairs of opposites, there is only Absolute Unity. So how do we harmonize a pair of opposites (like different cultures or groups) that we come across in day-to-day life? This needs creativity. If you are in the company of two friends of opposite views, how can you please both of them and not antagonize either of them? How can you be like a rose that everyone appreciates?

One possible answer is to say nothing and therefore offer no outward sign of favoritism. Perhaps this is where the term "silence is golden" is truly appreciated. Also silence allows a person to reflect and often find an answer within. If I do not know how to harmonize, I should give myself some time to think deeply on the matter and find a creative solution.

Another response could be to find a solution away from the two opposite views. In academic life, there is a thesis to a proposal or observation and its opposite, called the antithesis. There is also a synthesis, which is the blending of both points of view. But in finding a synthesis one ultimately does not destroy the basic concept of the thesis or the antithesis; rather one punctuates where there is truth in both. The psychologist Carl Jung was a great fan of synthesis, in part from his exposure to Eastern philosophy where he learned (from Buddhism) the concept of encouraging patients to harmonize two psychic opposites. With this harmonization the patient could coexist with himself and what Jung referred to as his "shadow self" or the dark side of his personality. I recall Joseph Campbell talking about Jung and describing Jung's views about the *chakras* of *kundalini* yoga. Jung thought that the West might only be about the level of the third or fourth chakras, whereas the East, in Jung's view, was far advanced. Culmination occurs at the seventh chakra. Jung would also prescribe for patients or individuals to harmonize with society, and society with Nature, as a means of finding a peaceful coexistence of opposites. Note that society does not blend into Nature nor does Nature blend into society. Rather the truth of Nature and its principles become an example to society and the individual of the journey they are on through life. Nature in fact teaches and instructs and therefore enlightens and helps one to transcend.

Mahatma Gandhi saw teaching as a key to enlightenment and transcendence. *Satyagraha*, non-violent resistance, had as its goal the desire to change the oppressor by not resisting him but by transforming him through action that would make him reflect on what he was doing. From Gandhi's perspective, both the British and the Indians were of opposite cultures that could actually learn from one another, journey together but still remain uniquely separate. Gandhi ultimately helped achieve independence by convincing the British that colonialism was evil, helping them transcend to a higher level.

Perhaps what puzzled the British was how such a diverse nation as India could rule itself and keep the integrity of its various unique regions, customs, dialects and religions. This is still one of the marvels of India.

Let us talk of two extreme opposites—good and evil. How do we harmonize them? For example, in Gandhi's view, colonialism was, though evil, due to ignorance. India, South Africa, and many other nations got their independence without war but by education and pressure based on world opinion. Southern states in the USA were ruled by segregationists and the Ku Klux Klan. Today, they have been replaced by democratically elected government, with whites, Latinos and African Americans sharing power. However, there are many mythic and historical stories, like those of the *Ramayana* and World War II, when force was necessary to defeat evil.

There may be differences of opinion on what is good and what is evil. My perception of good is that it always goes through sub-ration and transcendence toward the Ultimate, the light of knowledge and wisdom, like a flowing river, never stagnant, always moving toward the ocean. Evil regresses or stays stagnant, corroded, and becomes cancerous. I am optimistic about the future since evolution allows us to be more organized and better prepared amid diminishing resources. Based on recent research, genetically we are embedded with faith, and based on the findings of Will Durant, we will always progress toward the Ultimate, whatever that Ultimate may be.

Descartes and the Existence of God

Descartes was among the first few in the West responsible for building the bridge between the mind and the body. His contribution in the field of science and philosophy was separating and defining both mind and body. He was able to distinguish mind, unlike matter, as non-local (it does not have any location in space), not divisible, and existing independently of matter. Matter, unlike mind, is divisible and has a location. This separation of body and mind has been described in Eastern traditions thousands of years back even more clearly.

But Descartes also made profound blunders like the blunder of making consciousness the property of mind. The implication here is that he believed in upward causation, meaning matter was first, mind second, and the last was consciousness. Eastern traditions believe in downward causation where consciousness that is Brahman (God) is the highest state of being, followed by the mind and the body that is matter. His second blunder was to believe that the non-material world, though separate, interacted with the localized material world. It reminds me again of the story from *Reader's Digest* given at the end of chapter 4, about scientists in USA trying to see if the escaping soul can be detected.

People who are agnostic or atheist should consider following a few signs of the Divine.

As explained in Chapter 3, Ruta is the first evolute, the first cause, the first sign of the Absolute and Samskara acquired through hard training becomes the first link, the first several steps to transcend to the ultimate state of Godhood.

If we believe in downward causation, we have to believe in God. Downward causation occurs in a non-ordinary, non-local state of consciousness that we call "God-consciousness."

If we believe that we have a soul (*Atman*), then we have to believe in God (*Brahman*).

If we accept that we have the power of creativity, then we must accept the existence of God.

Creativity often is instantaneous and spontaneous because we are connected with consciousness. Ruta and samskara are very much instrumental to experience creativity.

If we accept the non-local non-ordinary working of quantum physics, we are indeed a lover of God.

Only downward causation can help us resolve the mystery of fossil gaps in the theory of evolution.

The fact that we perceive, communicate, and understand each other is due to our connection to consciousness. If we believe that mind could help heal the body, then consciousness is the cause. If the reader is interested in discovering more in detail, the reader should consider reading the book, *The Signatures of the Divine*, written by Professor Amit Goswami, and the poem *Whisper* given just before Chapter 1. As explained in Chapter 3, Einstein's insight of connecting the unchanging nature of light with the traditional view of the first glimpse of the Absolute, I believe, is one of the strongest proofs of the existence of the Absolute.

If we believe in Humanism, then certainly God loves us all. Following is a very appropriate poem written by James Henry Leigh Hunt.

ABU BEN ADHEM

Abu Ben Adhem
(may his tribe increase!)
Awoke one night from a deep dream of peace,
And saw, within the moonlight in his room,
Making it rich, and like a lily in bloom,
An angel writing in a book of gold:
Exceeding peace had made Ben Adhem bold,
And to the presence in the room he said,

"What writest thou?"

The vision raised its head,
And with a look made of all sweet accord,
answered, 'The names of those who love the Lord.'

'And is mine one?' said Abu.

'Nay, not so,'
replied the angel.

Abu spoke more low,
But cheerily still; and said,
'I pray thee then,
Write me as one that
loves his fellow men.'
The angel wrote, and vanished.

The next night
It came again with a great wakening light,
And showed the names whom love of God had blessed,
And lo! Ben Adhem's name led all the rest.

—*James Henry Leigh Hunt*

Chapter 7
Culmination and Vision at a Glance through Aphorisms

Unity—Its Why, What and How

We come now to the end of a journey—or is it the beginning of another one? Here we take steps toward an understanding of the goal of the endeavor, the details of which we have examined. The question before us is, what is the ultimate human goal? If I answer, unity, I need to explain what unites and how unity can be reached.

If one looks at life clearly, one sees that the ultimate human goal is always the unity of everything—the unity of fundamental sciences, natural forces; and the unity of humanity based on two evolutions, external and internal. But as we try to unify, we struggle with a diversity of beliefs, cultures, and values. Is the glass half-full or half-empty? Are we progressing or regressing? I suppose part of humanity will progress and part will regress and there will always be chaos and order generated out of it. That is the fundamental character of Nature. There are always going to be differences of opinion and custom. The East, more so than the West, recognizes that multiple pairs of opposites exist and need to be kept in balance and harmony.

Ironically, the origin of science seems to be at odds with the concept of unification because science has been based on reductionism as its approach to Nature. How can an approach based on division bring unity of the four fundamental forces? Author Rupert Sheldrake, who, as a scientist, tried to combine science and spirituality, has challenged reductionism. He once commented that he felt it was tragic he had to learn about the plants that he loved by cutting them up and killing them. Sheldrake, who received his Ph.D. in biology from Cambridge and studied philosophy at Harvard, was deeply influenced by his stay and study in India, where he lived for seven years and developed ways of seeing science and spirituality as compatible concepts.

India was a fertile field for this, and he admits living in India helped him to discover the concept of the "morphic field." This is a term, employed by Sheldrake, for a mysterious connection between people, animals, plants, and the universe. For example, Sheldrake observed that the DNA in previous species of tigers influences later tigers on the planet through the morphic field. A rat trained to walk through a cage will influence a rat 3,000 miles away that has not been exposed to similar training nor had any way to communicate with or learn from the laboratory-trained rat. Two groups of termites will start to dig separate nests and meet at the same location in what Sheldrake believed was the morphic field. Other instances can be found in our experiences, when people sense they are being stared at from behind (by someone who actually is), or when homing pigeons impressively find their destinations without previously knowing the route.

Ultimately Sheldrake came to the conclusion that reductionism has inhibited mankind from appreciating the wonders of Nature. I would agree. To help bring about unity in the world, we need to move away from reductionism toward unification. But how do we approach unification in a world filled with so many differences of opinion, values, and motives? From the Eastern perspective, we find an answer in the philosophy of accepting the whole with both its opposites, good and evil. Recall that from an Eastern perspective, bad is not bad but ignorance; bad is the raw material for good.

As our evolution on earth toward unity progresses, so do many facets of truth. Coal under severe pressure becomes a diamond after thousands of years. So, too, we as human beings need to develop on the path of life, taking negative things in our personalities and the environment and refining them into the diamonds that they can become. Concepts of revolution, riots, and economic market crashes represent chaos or negativity. But just as God (*Brahman*) created the universe out of chaos, these negativities are foundations of the higher order of enlightened truths. By employing both reductionism and integration in our approach to life (the allopathic and ayurvedic or the Western and Eastern approaches), we can accelerate a higher order in non-scientific fields.

In mathematics, for instance, we speak of opposites in terms of digital (arithmetic) and analog (geometric). To solve mathematical problems on a large scale, we often employ both concepts. An artist would say that the world is in an analog stage, emphasizing that the human mind is used more for understanding, grasping, absorbing, and acquiring information analogically rather than digitally. Remember the saying, "A picture is worth a thousand words?" A picture is a display of information analogically, while the words or captions beneath it can be counted and are therefore digital. Pictures and words, the analog and the digital, are pairs of opposites, but they work together to inform and educate. Notice that two opposites don't have to be equal. And, in point of fact, good and evil are not equal, although I suspect that perceived good is in greater demand than perceived evil.

Yet to achieve the ultimate good, how do we combine these two reductionist and integrating approaches? In ancient Vedic teaching, *Ruta* (the essence of Nature) and *Samskara* (the essence of humanity) are both seen as having value and purpose. *Samskara* guides the total human self—somatic, psychic, and spiritual—to unify, using Nature as a model. Yet each domain of the self is not eliminated or combined with the others, but operates in collaboration with them. This collaboration is an excellent model for the future unity of people, nations, and the world. Through positive effort and mental and spiritual training, *Samskarics* have a better chance of unifying the whole of humanity.

Mental attitude is important in the process. *Samskara* can encourage positive thinking as one sub-rates and transcends to higher levels of the self.

Humanity has recognized the selflessness of saints and sages. A selfless saint has lost his identity and is unified with Nature, or he has become Nature. Stated differently, the experiencer of unification is the saint who has lost his identity by becoming selfless. Most do not know that the saint is selfless, since the saint without an identity cannot communicate about himself to others. Others cannot know the saint is selfless, since they have no knowledge or experience of being selfless. Few may be able to recognize that the saint is selfless or close to being selfless due to their own experience of the saint's actions.

Bound to Historicity, Self-Centered Conditioned Mind

Figure 7-1b Saving us from ourselves by transcending from the self-centered somantic to the psychic to the egoless selfless state, merging with nature.

The Holy Grail in science is to discover the theory of unification of the four fundamental forces of Nature. Scientists have had some success in unifying three forces, but not the fourth. They have been successful in discovering the smallest sub-atomic particles, like quarks and neutrinos, employing the approach of reductionism and machines like atom smashers and particle accelerators. It is an approach based on division and separation. Such an approach is the opposite of that of integration and unification. Besides, an analytical approach ends up in discontinuous singularity that becomes difficult to analyze logically. However, the approach of reductionism has brought us the knowledge of the smallest sub-atomic particles, bringing us closer to the Nothingness that is Sunyata and Nirguna Brahmana articulated by scholars of Buddhism and Advaita Vedanta.

It is possible that this approach could induce the mind of a scientist to the experience of unification with Nature via a spontaneous mental jump analogous to a "quantum leap" as occurs in sub-atomic particles. However, the scientist may not be able to describe or theorize the process of unification. If ever a scientist claims success in theorizing the unification of the four fundamental forces of Nature, it would have to include an element of his indescribable experience of unification.

There are moments, even hours, of becoming selfless for some—for example, a musician or a vocalist, immersed in their music and their art. They lose their identity and become sound waves of the music, ever expanding and becoming one with the listeners and Nature around them. It could happen to anyone involved in selfless activities of goodness.

Unification with Nature or unification of anything, including the four forces of Nature, requires the experience of the total human self with each faculty, including the intellect, in harmony and balance with the rest.

The only way to unify in such a diverse Nature is through the process of transcendence that could bring the experience of Unity by becoming selfless. Selfless implies there is no ego and no mental mass, therefore no inertia, analogous to the transformation of a sub-atomic particle to an ever-expanding wave with infinite agility. The self-centered mind, as Thomas Kuhn makes his case about individual and cultural relativism with respect to science, can never discover absolute truth (figure 7.1).

Morphic Fields and Human Togetherness

Mental attitude is so important that film director David Lynch and former Ziff-Davis executive Robert Brown have proposed to raise one billion dollars to build meditation centers. They want to demonstrate the practicality of their belief that transcendental meditation can reduce urban stress and foster world peace. As Lynch has pointed out, it has been conclusively demonstrated by some 52 published studies on meditation and peace, and by what is known as the "technology of consciousness," that positive meditation by large masses of people can reduce crime and war casualties. The National Institute of Health has recently granted more than 20 million dollars to study TM's effect on heart disease. Researchers at the Maharishi International University in Fairfield, Iowa, have even demonstrated a connection between large numbers of people meditating together and a reduction in the "misery index," which is the sum of inflation, interest, and unemployment rates. Sheldrake himself theorized that a scientist's attitude toward an experiment would affect the results, positively or negatively.

Our mental attitude does affect our ability to unify, and *Samskara* helps our mental ability. Experts associated with Maharishi Institute's findings, are convinced that if enough people pray and wish for peace there will be peace, thanks to the morphic field that has been created.

Ashish Nandi, an Indian philosopher and Gandhian, has proposed a theory of ethical cycles. It states that anything good done or bad inflicted by one nation or group to another, in the economic or political field, returns to the giver or the inflictor in a cyclical movement of history. This theory apparently is based on the concept of karma yoga, one of the paths to salvation. It seems to support the idea of positive or negative thinking, applying the well-known Newtonian "equal action and reaction" to the field of economics. According to Nandi, the American standard of living peaked in the 1970s and began to decline thereafter. Nandi also pointed out that the West exported opium to China in the past and now the East exports drugs to the West. Did the standard of living decline because of the negativity of mass Iranian protests against the United States where a whole nation was praying and saying, "Death to America"? Did the Soviet Union ultimately collapse because millions of Catholics prayed for the conversion of Russia for over 50 years? And was America's wealth and prosperity blessed ultimately because of all the good America has performed for humanity? I believe the greatness of America is due to the positive attitude of its people.

This brings us back to good old reductionist science and Newton's natural law where equals and opposites play out. Can a massive population create a morphic field of hate or love? And does love heal the lover just as hate hurts the hater? I would argue that what is true on an individual basis is also true on a mass social and national scale, and vice versa. If a person wishes ill of another he will suffer ultimately, catching the individual in his own net. This is played out in the Indian mythic story of King Dasratha and young Shravana, who was taking his parents on a pilgrimage when the king inadvertently but carelessly caused his death. Shravana's parents, dying through grief of the loss, cursed the king, causing him to die, like themselves, with the pain of separation from his own beloved son in his heart.

We underestimate how connected we are to each other and how we can, through trained thinking and looking to Nature as a guide for our path to spiritual truth, ultimately unify our world. One sees the signs, visually, of world peace. It is not as crazy an idea as we might think. Our mental attitude and our acceptance of good as well as evil, and seeing evil as something that can be transformed into good, is part of the path. During the 1969 flight to the moon, when the controller at the Houston space center asked Neil Armstrong who was navigating the Apollo spacecraft, he blithely replied, "Newton." Armstrong clearly was saying that Nature and God were working together to do something wonderful and historical—walking on another planet and coming back to earth safely. In that case it was the moon. Imagine what other things we can achieve when we combine our spirituality with science. Peace on the moon, or maybe even on the earth.

Inheritance and Cultivation

We have seen that the somatic self has two aspects, the body and genes. Similarly, the psychic self has two aspects, intuition and intellect. The question we have to ask is whether these four are conditions imposed on the total human self, or are they, too, material to be educated, trained, cultivated, and transcended? My perception in this matter is not ambiguous; it is clear to me that no matter what kind of genes, body or psyche we inherit or are born with, the aim of life is to obtain *Samskara* by culturing and training whatever comes to us as an inheritance or a gift from a source beyond us. But the million dollar question is: How do we educate ourselves to become truly *Samskaric*? How do we cultivate to their finest perfection, within human limits, all our God-given equipment?

Again, my answer to this all important question comes without hesitation. This cultivation, the creation of *Samskara*, which relates us to *Ruta*, the first evolute and the best of Nature, can be made possible during the early stages of our life through right education and cultivation with toughness but plenty of love from teachers and parents. Toughness and discipline without love can be disastrous. A much greater proportion of love and care for a child is required than discipline. Failure or neglect in this, under whatever pretext, proves to be too painful later for the adult. It is here that the careful experiments and precise tools and methods created by the ancient sages and *rishis* of the East could help save man in the modern world.

This wisdom is not confined to the East. In fact an excellent and celebrated example of *Samskara* is that of Helen Keller and her teacher Anne Sullivan. The somatic self of the child Helen Keller had a deficiency that could have rendered her world lightless and soundless forever. But her teacher helped her cultivate the tips of her fingers to do the work of her eyes and ears, with love and firmness. In human history, this is not an isolated instance. There are many such stories, which show that *Samskara* and *Ruta* make all the difference in human life to bring the ultimate goal within reach.

Another example is that of Tony Menendez who migrated as a child from Guatemala to the USA with his family. Due to a birth defect, the boy had no hands. But neither the child nor his parents and teachers gave up. Tony learned to play the guitar with his toes. He and his teachers took pains to see that Tony was not an ordinary guitar player. Through hard training and application, he became such a good guitar player that he was invited to play for Pope John Paul II when the Pope visited Tony's part of the world. The Pope was so overwhelmed that he could not stop hugging him. Disabled people who achieve are to be admired so much more.

Expansions—Outward and Inward

Cultivation and education bring with them an impressive expansion of human capabilities, both somatic and psychic. The implications of such expansion, especially in our own time, are truly amazing and double-edged.

Hence, we have to face up to an important question, which we tend to shy away from: Why is inward expansion more important today than ever before? Imagine what could happen to Nature or Mother Earth if external growth keeps rising with more polluting, gas-consuming SUVs, Hum-Vees, and power plants.

The remarkable global phenomenon of rising income in developing countries with little education has accelerated population growth. This could create more "human tsunamis" since Nature will never allow man to be her master. Education could help to control population.

The cultivation of human tools, physical and intellectual, can be a good thing. But there is a simple condition attached to that goodness: education, *Samskara*, is the direction needing to be expanded in the journey of mankind. Here the ancient wisdom of mankind, cultivated so carefully and painstakingly in the East, steps in. It draws our attention to the other side of the expansion of human capabilities, the inward expansion, which Sri Aurobindo called involution.

Inward expansion is a good solution for man to grow, disturbing Nature less. The psychic self closer to divinity needs to be cultivated and cultured. The journey of life has to be toward the "poetic" philosopher-self at the doorstep of spirituality, through detachment, sub-ration, and transcendence for unity.

Steps toward Cultivation—Introspection and Meditation

To be non-judgmental is not at all the same as to be passive or inactive—quite the contrary. It involves the purest and most intense of all activities, indeed, a process of such activities. I have earlier identified these as clustering, detachment, sub-ration, evolution, and transcendence. Now is the time and place to ask what the engine is that energizes and runs this process. How are the activities that empower an individual and a nation to transcend in this journey of the total human self?

The most tested and trusted means has been the way of introspection and meditation. They are the vehicles of choice for transcendence to higher levels of consciousness. Though the origin of meditation, I suspect, is in India, it has been accepted and practiced in many faiths. Joseph Campbell stated that Christianity was born out of meditation in the first millennium.

Meditation allows one to become a witness to one's parade of conditioned thoughts and feelings. Desires and historical memories are hurdles that disrupt the process of meditation. Meditation has, unfortunately, been unnecessarily mystified and seen as a means for occult powers in several religious traditions. What then is the objective of meditation? Introspection and meditation are closely interlinked and have a pure and liberating effect of "thought-lessness," out of the space-time continuum. Joseph Campbell compares such a state of mind to a pond of water with no ripples whatsoever; here the ripples are analogous to streaming thoughts.

In a dialogue with physicist David Bohm, J. Krishnamurti describes the process of becoming thoughtless something like this: Each aspect of our human equipment needs to be active. Intellect directs the mind to be at attention, without any center of focus or direction. The process becomes timeless, the individual self does not exist and becomes selfless, and the brain has no historicity, no memory, no images, and no thoughts. The individual consciousness merges into the Universal Consciousness, with a perception of being one with the Universal Self. There is an experience of an explosion of love but without a perceiver; there is also an experience of blissful silence and unchanging infinitely spacious Consciousness. It would have to be a spontaneous process to come out of the time domain.

There are two domains of philosophical thinking—on Nature and on the self within. It is the second domain in which philosophical thinking is at its subtlest. Philosophy of the psychic self studies the mind through introspection including meditation as employed by Eastern mystics and psychologists. There are various Western models, besides behaviorism, that include, for example, Freud's model dominated by unconscious drives.

When Eastern and Western models of philosophical thinking on the inner nature are juxtaposed, it can be observed that there are two extremes, based on studies of the psychic self: one is highly conditioned, self-centered, and self-aware, closer to the somatic self. The other focuses more on the unconditioned or less-conditioned psyche transformed into the poetic philosophic self at the doorstep of the spiritual domain associated with an experience of Universal Awareness. It involves experience but without ego, and awareness without exclusive self-awareness.

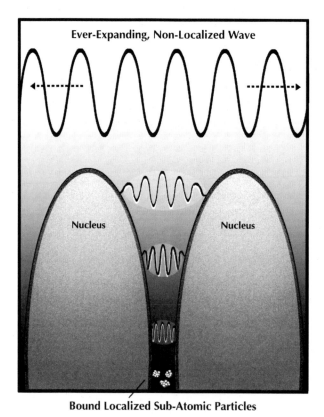

Figure 7-1a Transcendence of bound, localized sub-atomic particles to an ever-expanding non-localized wave (field).

As described by the eminent scientist and educator Dr. Kothari, this is analogous to the two states of sub-atomic particles, either as a local, deterministic particle or a non-local, ever-expanding, unifying wave. A non-local psyche would have transpersonal experiences, for example, simultaneous discoveries of Nature and paranormal telepathy of the kind described by Rupert Sheldrake as the morphic field. Soul (*Atman*) is our substratum connected to the Supreme Being (*Brahman*); *Brahman* is the Cosmic Consciousness and the cause of all existence as described in Eastern scriptures. Christianity refers to this primary consciousness as the Holy Spirit. Some Buddhist philosophers call it "No Self," similar to *Nirguna Brahmana*. Assagiol, a modern psychologist, has referred to this "No Self" or selfless self as the transpersonal self. Layers of consciousness, self-consciousness, and universal consciousness are the extremes. In monastic idealism, Adi Shankara has described consciousness as "one without a second." However he describes the layers representing various stages of development. The higher we develop, the more egoless we become, through the process of sub-ration and transcendence. Such an egoless consciousness is the true objective of all the tools and processes of human evolution.

One can compare over time the facial expressions of two types of humans—one who is self-centered, with affluence and power, and one who is selfless, like Buddha or Christ. One set of expressions would reveal extreme stress, while that of the selfless saint would radiate bliss and ecstasy. The best that can happen in one life is to first form a strong self-identity, with admiration and recognition of accomplishments in one's chosen fields from one's fellow men, and then transcend toward becoming selfless, losing that strong identity. It is the longest ascending path from stress toward happiness, but would result in acquiring permanent bliss. The author is convinced that any of us can achieve the state of selflessness—the state of Godhood.

From Cultivation to Culmination

The final step in this journey toward the culmination of egoless awareness involves an event the thought of which we tend to flinch from—the event of death. We know that for transcendence we need not fear death. Otherwise, regression and the fear of death could be compared to a tangled hierarchy depicted by a snake biting its own tail, as discussed in detail by physicist Amit Goswami in his book, *The Self-Aware Universe*. Another example is the American civil war when America was fighting with itself.

Is it possible to see death as a culmination, and perhaps as a doorway? Could death be considered as transcendence, about which we have been talking?

What is death and dying? When you are born, you cry but the world rejoices. But when you die, you rejoice but the world cries. Those are the words in *The Tibetan Book of the Dead*. To me, the Tibetan Buddhist concept of death is attractive. They believe that when I die, I will face a bright light and try to hold it. If I succeed, I do not come back. Light has been associated closest to God in almost every tradition. I have argued in the previous chapter that the light is the first glimpse of God based upon Einstein's assumption that the only unchanging and "Absolute" in his theory of relativity is the light; every thing else in nature is relative and changing.

Higher beings are portrayed in movies like *The Abyss*, starring Ed Harris, as if they are a source of light and glowing. The sun in the Upanishads is described as Sutratma that like a needle pierces all the jivatmas (life souls). The life soul, that is the individual self, has to realize its oneness with the cosmic wind and the sun. Unless it does so, it cannot cross the frontiers of death; it cannot know Immortality, so say the Indian scriptures. One who enters the door of the sun enters into Immortality, for beyond the sun is the realm of Immortality. However, as shown in Figure 7-2, God's light would have to be a lot brighter and faster with infinite speed than we experience in Nature, which is confined to the past and future space-time cones. The implication is that death is *mukti,* release from bondage. Death is part and parcel of transcendence and an opportunity. One should not fear death but welcome it.

Many traditions consider a sacrifice of death as an honor, bliss. Some outstanding examples of this exist from different cultures of mankind. The Japanese samurai accepted death as an honor, as a moral and ethical duty, as dharma. There are stories of native Indians facing a shower of bullets from General Custer's army while defending their families and territory, without showing pain because they thought the sacrifice was noble. A Buddhist monk in Saigon immolates himself as a sacrifice to protest against the Vietnam War, showing no sign of pain. The pain to the viewers when it was shown on American television was the start of soul-searching in America and a change in direction.

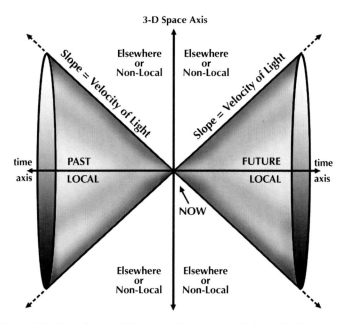

Figure 7–2 All attributes of Sahguna Brahman are infinite. In the space/time diagram, the existence of Nature is confined within two cones; however, Brahman exists everywhere including elsewhere (non-local) in this four dimensional space since Brahman's movement is with infinite velocity.

I would say that the supreme task before our philosophical self is to transform physical death into philosophical death. Philosophic death occurs when we move from one layer of existence to the next. Recall that Nature is fractal, that is, with multiple layers. When a dependent child grows up and becomes an independent, responsible adult who marries and has children of his own, the child in him dies, philosophically. When a woman becomes a mother, she sacrifices her own needs for those of the newborn child. Ancient sages of India have described a woman who has achieved motherhood as the goddess of love, since her love for her child is infinite. She is the goddess of patience, since she shows the utmost patience when the child is slow to learn during the growing-up period. She is the goddess of forgiveness, since she forgives the child's undesirable behavior and keeps encouraging improvement.

An inspiring story is told about a mountaineer Aron Ralston, who got stuck between a rock and hard place, literally, for a whole week with little water and a pocket knife. With his right arm pinned in a three-foot-wide opening, he used his engineering skill and the pocketknife to amputate his arm to free himself from a boulder weighing 1,000 pounds. In one way, he cheated certain death. However, he considered that he had died and been reborn without one arm and with a stronger body—this illustrates a philosophic death and rebirth.

The somatic self dies philosophically when the psychic self is born; though the body is alive, its only function is to support the psychic self. Death in the Vedic/Buddhist tradition is a mere change of clothes, the body being analogous to a garment. A change of garments, from soiled to clean, is indeed a matter for joy, not lamentation.

Evolution to the Spiritual Self: A Table

We have discussed throughout this book, and especially in this final chapter, what could be the ultimate objective of our total hu-

Table 7-1 Evolutionary Hierarchy towards the Spiritual Self — Evolution in Time				
Human equipment	Somatic (genetic and body)	Psychic (intuitive and intellectual mind)	Spiritual	Perception and concept of realm of Brahman/God, the Ideal, permanent
Definition and perception of belief	Nature within space/time matter/energy	Non-material but natural in the space/time of consciousness	Self-aware and believer in the Universal Conscious Mind	All-pervading Everywhere and Everywhen including "Elsewhere"
Process of detachment, sub-ration, and then transcendence to next level	Time-bound order; birth, growth, then decay and death; (Buddha) prepsychic, *Samskaric* development	Natural energetic unidirectional process of sub-ration; but increasing psychic order; desire to unify with ideal philosophical self	Transcendence to ideal spiritual self; a state of *Sat-Chit-Ananda* connected to Universal Mind	Constant unchanging Infinite Order or Nothingness *(Sunyaya)*
Time domain	Time-bound, non-permanent	Time-bound, non-permanent	Mentally timeless, connected to the whole	Ideal, timeless
End state	Decayed to zero order; maximum entropy, zero information	Non-existent at the end	Merged with ideal Ultimate *Samadhi*	Unchangeable infinite order; end does not exist
World view	Pythagorean Newtonian Laplacian	Heraclitean, Einstein, Gandhi	Buddha, Christ, Adi, Shankara, Rama, Krishna	Nirvana, Father-God, Mahesh, Moksha, Vishnu
Contribution of sages and scholars	Karl Marx, Gandhi	Freud, Einstein, King David, Jung	Christ, Moses, Buddha	Yahweh, Makom, Brahman, Nirvana, Sunyata

man self, and how that objective can be realized in the domains of the somatic, psychic, and spiritual selves. These three domains have been perceived as autonomous yet interconnected through a careful evolutionary process involving clustering, detachment, sub-ration, and adequate preparation within each domain for the evolutionary journey to the next domain.

Such an evolution takes place in time and has its own hierarchy, leading toward freedom or *mukti*, not merely physical death and the annihilation of the self. To be of use to readers, I have condensed this into a table, with the different categories under discussion placed in clearly visible interrelationships.

The table includes three columns for each layer of the total human self—somatic, psychic, and spiritual; the last column describes the human perception of the ideal. In Chapter 5 it was briefly discussed that more often clusters in Nature occur in two pairs or four elements, and clusters of five do occur as stated with a few examples. The same could be said even for the human total self if a state of mind was included that has transcended beyond the human psyche. When each of the four elements of the human self is in perfect balance and harmony with its opposite and with the other two, the human self of four tends to transcend into a state of perfection. One could say that the fifth element added to the four is the state of selflessness, the state that is in essence beyond nature and cannot be communicated and is yet to be realized.

The column of the somatic self connects the physical body and genetics to Nature and their interaction. Prince Siddhartha observed the stages of the human body as it declines and, after years of searching and a grueling existence, he transformed into Buddha. Karl Marx's message of taking care of the somatic self is important.

The third column describes the non-material interaction of the psychic self with Nature. However, the objective of the psychic self is clearly to be a bridge between the physical somatic self and the sublime spiritual self.

Not much is known about the spiritual self other than a few words from those who have experienced a state that can be described as "being spiritual." I would argue that the state of the spiritual self cannot be intellectually described other than using words like "a state of being blissful."

The last column is our human perception of an ideal. It has been described in Vedic scriptures as what the ideal is not, since it lies beyond our human sensory perception.

Ancient Wisdom and Contemporary Challenges

Ancient Indian sages were compassionate and understood the many limitations of the common man not only in their own times but for the future. One of the limitations that they seem to have anticipated is that of our attention span. Hence, *rishis* and sages distilled their vast wisdom and brilliant vision into brief but resonant statements in that great language, Sanskrit. These are *Mahavakyas* or Great Sentences or statements, saying much in a few words.

In this concluding and culminating section, I present ancient *Mahavakyas*, and as a humble tribute to my readers offer some aphorisms. They sum up my perception of the challenges of our own times and the answers that the wisdom of the ancients, together with the current knowledge of science, provide, if they are studied actively and diligently by us in our own context.

First, the ancient *Mahavakyas*:

Mahavakyas of the Spiritual Self

1. *Pragnanam Brahma*: Consciousness is *Brahman*.

(*Rig Veda*) Individual Mind is connected to Universal Mind.

2. *Tat twam asi*: That thou art (*Sama Veda*).

The total human self is essentially Divine.

3. *Ayam Atman Brahma*: The total human self is *Brahman* (*Arthavana Veda*).

4. *Aham Brahma asmi*: I am *Brahman* (*Yajur Veda*).

Conclusion: Our sub-stratum, our foundation, our consciousness is connected to *Brahman*, the Universal Mind; therefore we are essentially Divine.

To interpret this ancient and eternal wisdom in terms of our contemporary world, with its problems and challenges, aspirations and opportunities, and to distill my own perceptions presented throughout this book, I offer the following aphorisms.

Vision at a Glance through Aphorisms

• Total selves (organisms) are autonomous, self-organizing, and ceaselessly exchange matter and energy with Nature. Nature and the total human self coexist and are symbiotic. Knowledge of Nature helps man to discover the solution to human problems. However, Nature will never be a slave of man.

• Not only total human selves but also organizations, including economic markets, are natural; they all have somatic and psychic needs. Their attributes are similar everywhere.

• Total human selves renew themselves through birth, death, and birth again, and contain attributes of all creatures. A total human self is a living museum of Nature. It contains the successes and failures of Nature. The goal of the total human self is to learn, evolve, and transcend to higher levels.

• The total human self operates linearly but often non-linearly and between extremes. It exists at different levels: somatic (body and genetics), psychic (intuitive mind and intellect), and spiritual. The psyche is the bridge between somatic and spiritual.

• The total human self is a world within a world. Total human selves and Nature are never disconnected from each other. Nature, in the language of mathematics, is fractal, like an onion. Nature displays a self-similar pattern of fractal geometry, the outer layer being the mother of the inner layer.

• The Gujarati folktale during the devotional period (about a millennium ago in India), called *"Pinde so Brahmande,"* conveys that whatever is in the somatic self is also in the cosmos.

• The total human self exists in a space constituted by multiple pairs of opposites. Boundaries of this space are dynamic and changing. Good and evil form a pair of opposites, where evil is inseparable from ignorance.

• The total human self must learn to find his/her multidimensional space and boundaries, unique for every individual, and learn to live close to the center. If one hits a boundary, one could perish. Boundaries are not fine lines of demarcation but a cluster of barriers, of different heights and widths, occupying a portion of the living space.

• The total human self, organisms, and organizations are orders with some disorder. Old orders decay and die and are replaced by newer orders. Species rise and disappear, as do empires.

• Outcomes in Nature are neither 100 percent certain nor perfect. The total human self, a part of Nature, is an order with some disorder generated out of chaotic Nature. There are many different orders but only one chaos.

• If God is unchanging and absolute, Nature is ever-changing and cannot be absolute, but is second only to God. Everything, including the books of knowledge, commandments, and discovered laws of Nature, could change in time.

• Hindsight is always 20/20; however Nature is 80/20. Events occur in clusters, things form clusters, and are almost never evenly distributed. Often the change occurs in jumps; when it rains it pours. Examples of clusters are: blood clots, stars, autos on the freeway, people of the same cultural background. Prices cluster around the mean.

• Autonomy of order at every level and layer probably prolongs the life of the order. Autonomy implies no external disturbance. Autonomy slows down the process of decay. An order that adapts to its environment also extends its life. The mixing of orders may accelerate the decay. The implication is that the somatic, psychic, and spiritual selves should never mix or interfere with each other.

• Time in Nature is relative, never absolute. When things happen in clusters, time accelerates. When nothing happens, there is boredom with no excitement. Then time almost stands still.

• Laws of Nature, organisms, total human selves, in fact information in general, are forms of order in a chaotic universe. Chaos by definition has zero information. There are desirable and undesirable orders in Nature. There are many orders but only one chaos. Knowledge is obtained from noise-infected information employing human intellect. Wisdom is derived from knowledge and from the experience of every human faculty, including an integrated psyche.

• Creative order-generating activity of the human mind is at least as significant as, if not more than, the natural evolutionary processes that give birth to the somatic self, mother of the human psyche.

• The outcomes of cultural evolution generated by organisms are less complex and less diverse than those generated by biological evolution. Cultural evolution is visible, knowable and occurs in a much shorter time span than invisible biological evolution.

• Biological, meaning somatic, evolution is natural, unpredictable, and not accessible to the psychic self. Cultural evolution and revolution is associated with the psychic self and is predictable; tools such as mathematics, language, and computers are employed for that purpose.

• Organisms, organizations, and markets evolve. Evolution implies long periods of equilibrium with short periods of quantum change, with increasing complexity. Human evolution helps to forecast turbulences, but never with certainty.

• A free market economic system, along with appropriate checks and balances, is probably the most natural compared to others, including socialism and communism. However it will keep changing, evolving, and adapting to its environment.

• One needs to cross the somatic boundary to enter into psychic space. This implies a philosophic death of the somatic self and the need to be reborn as the psychic self.

• There is always some good in the worst of us and some bad in the best of us. It is not meant for us to judge others. A "holier than thou" attitude creates more problems than solutions. A step toward human unity is to have every faith coexist with other faiths. Patchwork coexistence implies "unity in diversity."

• Within one's domain, one should be inclusive of others. The process of transcendence from the somatic to psychic to the philosophical self is unidirectional. Regression should be avoided though there are exceptions.

• Autonomy is the prerequisite to detachment. Detachment is the prerequisite to sub-ration, and sub-ration is the prerequisite to transcendence. The total human self needs to experience both transcendence and immanence.

• There is, in an idealized God's nature, an infinite quantity of information. However, the information accessible to the total human self is only that information that can come across and be observed by the equipment given to the total human self (Anthropic Principle). The total human self chooses what, why, and how to observe and interpret results.

• Four basic units of the total human self symbiotic with Nature are genetics, the physical body, the intuitive mind, and the intellectual mind; just as length, mass, time, ampere, and lumen are the basic units of measurement in physics. Components of every field of human endeavor can be connected to these four basic units of the total human self *(See Tables 1 to 5 at the end of chapter 5).*

• The somatic part of the total human self is like fish swimming in water having no predictable direction. It is the psychic self that establishes the type of order we associate with humanity. *Samskara* helps to guide the somatic and psychic selves to establish the order toward perfection.

• *Samskara* is a positive life-fulfilling spontaneity of the somatic self. Culturing and cultivating the thought-like urges and feelings of the somatic self result in *Samskaras*. *Maya* is the opposite of *Samskara*. *Maya* is the defamed trickster that tries to confuse the somatic self. Contrary to the Western belief of separated and unconnected good and evil, the Indian masters believe good and evil are connected and a pair of opposites, where evil is ignorance and good is knowledge and wisdom; where evil is the raw material of good.

• It is not correct to believe that the subconscious is the last labyrinth or maze. Deeper than the subconscious are the needs of survival—hunger, instinctive impulses and reactions.

• *Ruta* is the truth in creation. If *Brahman* is abstract, *Ruta* is Brahman's natural and material form and exists in all organisms. It can be known only through *Samskara*. *Ruta* is the first evolute and the essence of Nature.

• A strong will, persistence, endurance, resilience, and intuition are attributes of a *Samskaric* person, acquired through culturing and hard training of the somatic self.

• *Samskara* is the power and the feminine side of *Ruta*. *Ruta* operates and becomes functional only through *Samskara*. Experiencing the scent of the rose, and the joy of music, is because of *Ruta* and *Samskara*. *Samskara* is the cause of the dutiful soldier, the fiery flamenco dancer, and the inspiring speaker. A *Samskaric* person will not hurt, but will bring out the best mood, love, and truth in the people around him/her.

• Human impulses of sympathy, compassion, and non-violence are instinctive and spontaneous. They are the signs of being humane and *Samskaric*.

• Time heals all wounds applies to both the somatic and psychic selves. Physical wounds get cured due to the workings of the interior of the body. Psychological wounds get cured due to the workings of *Samskara* and the philosophical self.

• *Samskara* implies faith in the good, not necessarily faith in God. *Samskara* is associated first and foremost with the somatic self; it forms a bridge to the psychic and then to the philosophical self. Samskara is the first and foremost instrument for transcendence.

• One needs to put more emphasis on the positive and not the negative. The ancient Indians believed the greed of anything including wisdom is as harmful as the greed of gold. To gain wisdom, one has to die philosophically and be reborn in the psychic domain to transcend. Greed here implies attachment hindering detachment.

• There is no absolute determinism in a chaotic universe. All processes, including all scientific observations, are irreversible. One need not brood over the dead past, nor worry about the unborn future, but must act in the living present. Stated differently: Yesterday is history, tomorrow is mystery, and today is a gift; that is why it is called "the present."

• There is a quantum analog of the total human self, which exists as a self-centered individual and can transcend to a selfless non-local universal consciousness, just as a sub-atomic particle like an electron can transform from an individual particle to an ever-expanding and unifying wave of light. Becoming selfless has to be the ultimate goal in the life of every human being.

• The psychic part of the total human self produces discrete, indivisible, non-continuous thought jumps, just as sub-microscopic particles like electrons make quantum jumps. In both cases the act of observation will disturb the outcome.

• Earth is not only a living organism but is also self-aware, through all her living creatures, organizations, and financial markets. There are constant battles between these for the well-being of mother earth, just as there are battles of cells in the human body to survive and prosper.

• Expansion and clustering are common in Nature and in the human psyche. Astronomers accept galactic expansions as real; empires and corporations tend to expand. Our knowledge of Nature is expanding, even exploding, thanks to the external cultural evolution that includes high-tech homes, automobiles, telephones, and computers. Genetics connects all of us homo-sapiens in somatic realm, technology like telephones, internet and GPS system keep us connected in psychic realm.

• Free will and freedom to choose is a gift from Nature to humanity. However, this gift is relative in value. It cannot be absolute since Nature assures and guarantees the availability of an opposite to every dimension, even in matters of free will and the freedom to choose.

• Spontaneous creativity happens only when every faculty complements each of the others and works in harmony. An ideal and the creativity of the human mind is a bigger monument to Nature and God than a temple or a cathedral. However, there is creativity employed in building temples and cathedrals and they do have an important place in every society.

• The natural home of happiness is within the individual self. Once discovered within, it bridges the gulf between the total human self and Nature.

• Unity in the total human self within and with Nature is possible only if every self, every human faculty, including the intellect, complements each other and works in harmony with all the other selves, but never with only the intellect, and not by the reductionist approach of division.

Any of us can come close and even enter the state of selflessness or the state of divinity. Being selfless implies there is no fear of death and the mind becomes infinitely agile, like a wave of light. Light is the first glimpse of the Absolute. Becoming selfless has to be the ultimate goal for every human being.

Appendix 1
Ancient Prophecy and Darwin's Evolution

On the theme of evolution, I will juxtapose two well-known perceptions of this process. One is, of course, the famous theory of evolution presented by the scientist, Charles Darwin. Based on observation and analysis, he has shown how more complex organisms evolved from simpler ones, responding to the needs of survival. This upset the older Christian view on the subject.

The other is another perception, from the tradition of the Indian scriptures. *Vishnu Purana* is one of the major texts of the post-Vedic period. It is dedicated to Vishnu, the God of the sustenance of life. *Vishnu Purana* gives an account of ten incarnations of God. It is known as the *Dashavatara* narrative.

These *avataras* or incarnations are as follows:

1. *Matsya* is the first incarnation, perceived as a great horned fish. It is interesting to note that the fish is seen in stories of the origin of life, and in various cultures, as the one who saves life from a deluge of water.

2. *Kurma*, the second incarnation, is seen as a mighty turtle. It belongs to water as well as earth.

3. The third incarnation is *Varaha*, or *Maha-Varaha*. Perceived as a powerful and merciful great boar, he saves the earth from the bottom of chaos.

4. The fourth incarnation is a form that is half-man and half-lion. It is called *Narasimha*, literally man with a lion head. As Narasimha, God saves a devotee, Prahlada, from his own demonic father.

5. The fifth incarnation is known as *Vamana*, the small one or the midget. He turns from being a small one to the largest one, encompassing all the Three Worlds, and yet able to transcend.

6. The next incarnation is *Parasurama*, an angry sage, a contemplative man who brings the unruly political power to a rule according to ethical laws.

7. The seventh incarnation is that of *Rama*, the dutiful prince, who led the forces of good against the forces of evil, represented by King Ravana.

8. The eighth incarnation is that of *Krishna*. It is Krishna who, through the *Bhagavad Gita*, empowers man to take up the decisive fight against the rule of evil.

9. The Incarnation of Universal Compassion is universally known as *Buddha*, the Enlightened One.

10. The tenth incarnation, that has not yet happened, is supposed to be of *Kalki*. *Kalki* will bring life to a conclusion.

It is astonishing, when one looks at this chronology of ten *avataras* that it seems to fit with the succession of processes established by Darwin in his theory of evolution.

India and East Asia accepted the Buddhist ideals from the last *avatara* of God, from the time of their inception about 2,500 years ago. There are scholars who think that the ideals of Buddha and Christ are similar, if not the same. However, Buddhism did not spread in the West. Instead, a bifurcation occurred. First, Christianity was established as a state religion in Rome. Then Islam developed in the Middle East. Both claimed that their God was the only God who could bring salvation.

Today, it appears to me that the world is ready for one unified religion with multiple paths, that is, a patchwork of different paths.

Let us take an example of two opposites. Analysis, a reductionist approach, and synthesis, a holistic approach, are a pair of opposites. Both tools are needed and provide important application. Currently, the application of analysis outweighs the application of synthesis. We need to apply both tools with balance and harmony. Analysis is required to determine and distinguish two elements of a pair of opposites. However, the tools of synthesis help us to coexist and provide balance and harmony among multiple pairs of opposites. This is the essence of the ancient philosophy of Unity in Diversity or "there are many paths to the mountaintop" or *"Sarva dharma sama-bhava."* The meaning of the last statement is to give equal reverence to every path. These statements also imply non-judgment and autonomy to every domain of the self.

The political patchwork of coexistence can be achieved through the principles of *pancha sheela* originated by the former Prime Minister Jawaharlal Nehru of India, during the 1950s.

One could even consider integrating the best of all traditions. Could not a child grow up with the discipline and devotion as it is taught in Islam? Could not educated youth use the good work ethics and high aspiration practiced in the West? The Eastern traditions of Buddhism and Hinduism could possibly enter in later for the development of the inner self. I do not claim to be a scholar of any faith or belief system; I am a mere student of life. I believe, however, based on my experience, that extracting the best from every faith, every tradition, could uplift humanity and harmonize our selves with Nature.

Appendix 2
Will Durant's View on Human Progress, and Adi Shankara's Philosophy

Will Durant is best-known for his 11 volume masterpiece, *The Story of Civilization*, which took an unfathomable 50 years to complete. Throughout his long life, Durant somehow found time to write a number of other well-known books, emphasizing human progress.

What exactly is progress? After a great deal of written reflection, Durant defined it as the increasing control of the environment by man. He also referred to progress as the domination of chaos by the human mind and purpose and of matter by the human will. Durant listed, in the following order, what he believed to be the most important developments of man's climb from savage to scientist.

-Speech: Without words, there would be no philosophy, poetry, or history. Thoughts, at the highest level, would not exist.

-Fire and tools: This is the phenomenon that made possible tool making, cooking, and protection from climatic conditions.

-The conquest of animals: Durant reminded us that even though animals are now our playthings and our helpless food, there was a time of uncertainty whether man's brain would ultimately triumph over the brawn of beasts.

-Agriculture: Civilization, in his opinion, was not possible as long as men wandered as hunters. This change brought with it the idea of a permanent home.

-Social organization: This is the essence of the replacement of chaos with order. One could argue that the political and legal systems may be regressing more than progressing.

-Morality: Durant believed that man's character has probably retrogressed. Yet, he felt compelled to point out that we are slightly gentler than before. Durant did not live to see the current religious fanaticism and the Islamic jihad of the new millennium.

-Science: Durant referred to science as the victory of man over matter, but noted that it is not yet complete since man needs to control his faculties and expand within himself (This is part of the progress described as cultural evolution in Chapter 4).

-Education: Education, made possible by civilization, dramatically changed the notion of class by virtue of birth. The spread of mass education has moved at an accelerating pace, which in turn has changed the make-up of civilizations even more rapidly.

It is possible that we could retrogress if we are not careful to overuse the same tools that brought us to our current state. Buddha warned us on overusing words and speech, since speech together with intellect could make us devils, as happened during the first 50 years of the 20th century, a period of two world wars. The overuse of agricultural land, based on scientific research, could bring disaster in the future. We must not overlook our existence in a multidimensional space consisting of multiple pairs of opposites, as described by the ancient sages of India. We must be careful not to come too close to the opposite side of the boundary. Durant has warned us, on matters of morality, to be careful and progress within ourselves, so that we are victorious over ourselves.

Few of us can be certain of the true purpose of life, but thousands of years of human history make it apparent that man is programmed to move forward—to make progress. Unfortunately, only a small percentage of the world's population makes the greatest amount of progress *(See the 80/20 rule in Chapter 4)*. It is unlikely that anyone can individually do much to retard the progress of war, hunger, terrorism, or religious fanaticism—a few of the most common ailments. But we do have the capacity to make a difference individually in our own life.

I suspect what most people want is happiness. Some of the more obvious facets of life that lead to happiness are good health, wealth, purpose, love—and later on, graceful transcendence. Health, that is the somatic self, comes first, because without good health everything else is out of the picture. We know that to receive love, one has to give love. Idealists may not admit it, but the reality is that progress in resource building makes progress in the other areas of our lives much easier.

To make consistent progress, one has to become adept at controlling the chaos around us. A survivor is one who has learned to adapt to his environment. In today's world, chaos comes in many forms—a paucity of information in thousands of emails, telephone calls, and voicemail runarounds. Rapes, murders, acts of terrorism, and natural disasters are burdens that need to be reduced and ultimately removed. The challenge is to progress more rapidly as resourceful, healthy, loving, and focused human beings in the degenerated environment around us. Our time here on earth is limited. We need to use it wisely by focusing on making consistent progress in such areas as health, purpose, love and resources. By doing well in these areas, we can feel proud in the knowledge that we are among those individuals on this planet who are not adding to its problems.

Durant's View on Indian Philosophy

Will Durant, in Volume 1 of *The Story of Civilization*, describes Shankara as the greatest of Indian philosophers and compares him to Aquinas and Kant. Durant points out and observes the great wisdom of Shankara's Advaita, that it takes not only logic but also intuition and insight to grasp the essential out of the irrelevant, the eternal out of the temporal. Advaita Vedanta was interpreted by Adi Shankara during the

8th century A.D., and is expressed based on the author's interpretation in equation forms as follows:

G: God; M: Human self; D: Number of desires for himself, desires for possessions, hoarding, attachments; L: Man's pure unconditioned love; I: Infinity; R: degree of God-Realization; K: Constant; N = Number of incarnations

1. $G = M - D$; When $D = 0$, $G = M - 0 = M$;
2. When $D = I$, $N = I$;
3. When $L = I$, $M = G$;
4. $R = K/D$

In essence, man approaches Godhood when he approaches a state where he is at the verge of becoming self-less, and desire-less and feels infinite love for all.

The man who knew the mathematical face of God is a fascinating story of the brilliant, self-taught Indian mathematician, Srinivasa Ramanujan. It is also a history of the astonishingly fruitful cross-cultural collaboration between this young mathematical genius and his mentor at Cambridge University, G. H. Hardy—a relationship that turned the world of mathematics upside down. On matters of religion, Hardy has reported a statement of Ramanujan's to the effect that all religions are equally correct. Ramanujan credited his acumen to his family goddess, Namagiri, and looked to her for inspiration in his work. He often said, "An equation for me has no meaning, unless it represents a thought of God."

Based on an article in *Hinduism Today Magazine*, Ramanujan is supposed to have interpreted Brahman (B), the Absolute Reality, in both ways, as described by Adi Shankara.

Nirguna Brahman (Bn) was interpreted as Brahman of zero attributes (Xz) and zero manifestation (Yz), since none of them is observable by human faculties. It is also described as Sunyata or Nothingness. Sahaguna Brahman (Bm) is described as having infinite attributes (Xi) of infinite magnitude and has infinite manifestations (Yi).

In equation form:

Bm = Xi/Yi = Infinite/Infinite = 1 = Unity;

Bn = Xz/Yz = 0/0 = 1 = Unity = Bm = G

Appendix 3
Films that Reflect the Content of the Book

The author is describing and focusing on the message that comes out of each movie, based on all of its art and science, including the acting, the story, and the dialogue. The story could be fictional, the characters may not be real, but that is not important. For example, George Cohen in the movie *Yankee Doodle Dandy* is supposed to be a shady character in real life, which is not important here. The reader should focus on the content of the movie only.

Inherit the Wind (1960)

This film points out the extreme fanaticism of beliefs (the intuitive mind) and at the same time, intellectual arrogance. Historically, fanaticism of beliefs and tradition feeds on ignorance, and stifles intellectual pursuits. Liberty and freedom to choose is sacred, and should not be violated on any account. Today, the world has come a long way. "An idea-creating mind is a bigger monument than a cathedral," says Spencer Tracy, as an attorney defending the teacher of Darwin's theory of evolution. Brady, played by Fredric March, is the prosecuting attorney and a Bible scholar.

Two feuding parties fight over what constitutes truth, the Gospel or Darwin's theory. The problem even then was the bubbling arrogance of the intellectual press. Tracy lost the case in the lower court. However, at the end of the film, he articulates a statement about the opposing lawyer, Brady, after he collapses and dies, "Brady was a giant, but got lost (on the path of ignorance)." We need to remember that both fanaticism of faith, or for that matter of any field of human endeavor, and intellectual arrogance spring from ignorance.

Fanaticism of any blind belief or faith is the extreme, and the opposite of another belief that claims the absolute supremacy of intellectual reasoning. Intellect is not the highest human faculty because it associates itself with arrogance. It is an important human faculty, but it cannot have the absolute veto power of accepting or rejecting a belief. An integrated, balanced, and harmonized psyche with all its constituent components, including the intellect, would go beyond observation and reasoning.

The Mission (1986)

This historical drama of sweeping cinematic beauty is about an 18th-century Jesuit mission in the Brazilian jungle. The missionaries struggle against the legalized slave trade of Portugal and the politicized church. Somatic and spiritual Nazism is depicted in the film.

The scenery around Iguazu Falls in the Amazon jungle is spectacular. Father Gabriel, played by Jeremy Irons, brings the "golden age" to an Amazon Indian tribe, supported by Mendoza, a repentant former slave trader, played by Robert De Niro. The struggle of two opposites—the greed for gold for somatic needs and the total disregard for human brotherhood plays out against the idealism of the philosophical selves—has a tragic ending when ignorance defeats enlightenment.

The Miracle Worker (1962)

Teacher Anne Sullivan, played by Anne Bancroft, employs unconventional methods with "tough love" to help the deaf and blind Helen Keller, played by Patty Duke, adjust to the world around her. The film, an intense and moving experience, shows how the relationship is built between the teacher and the student.

In the film, the impulses and reflexes of the pre-psychic self, with little light within the somatic self, are trained and cultured. *Samskara* is brought in to uplift first the body, then the mind, and ultimately the soul. The film also shows how difficult it is for parents to watch their handicapped child going through disciplined training with occasional punishment, though the audience appreciates the outcome and admires the child's achievement.

My Left Foot (1989)

This biography is of cerebral-palsy victim Christy Brown, whose strong will and inborn *Samskara* overcome his handicap. He was considered an imbecile by everyone except his mother, until he teaches himself to write. He helps his family survive in impoverished Ireland by becoming a writer and painter of repute, employing his left foot, the only appendage over which he has control. Daniel Day-Lewis won an academy award, playing the part of Christy Brown.

Yankee Doodle Dandy (1942)

The story of George Cohen depicts a nostalgic view of the golden era of show business. His early days, triumphs, musicals, and romance are brought to life by the energetic superstar James Cagney in a rare and wonderful performance. Cagney was never more charismatic, dances fabulously, reportedly inventing the steps on the spot. The story happens at the time of the Second World War, and Mr. Cohen gets the chance to meet the president. "When a person like me gets to meet you, Mr. President, we must be doing alright. If I were you, Mr. President, I would not worry about us. We will do alright." The film shows tremendous positivism. A group, a society, or a country will do extremely well with such a positive attitude. Recall the advice of the Indian chief with two dogs encouraging the good dog more than the other.

The Bridge on the River Kwai (1957)

The film is an award-winning adaptation of the Pierre Bouelle novel about the battle of wills between a Japanese POW camp commander and a prisoner who is a British colonel, played by Alec Guinness, over the construction of a railway bridge. They represent a pair of opposites. It received many academy awards, including best film and best actor.

The Japanese army needed the bridge to transport war supplies to defeat the British and their allies. Guinness was trained as a soldier and believed in duty and honor. He sought better treatment for British soldiers from their Japanese captors, which happened when they agreed to build the bridge, using imagination, creativity, and craftsmanship. Mentally, the British were in the psychic domain, proud of the "masterpiece" they'd built. There was a sense of achievement and transcendence among the British soldiers. Guinness felt he was converting defeat into victory. He thought that, for years to come after the war, the bridge would bring a better life to the natives of Burma (now Myanmar), who would be grateful to the British soldiers. The British and Japanese, a pair of opposites, complemented each other in creating the bridge.

However, an escaped American soldier, played by William Holden, working with British commandos in hiding and set to destroy the bridge, could not understand what was going on in Guinness's mind. What was good for the Japanese was not good for the allies. The great powers of the time were fighting to preserve or expand their empires. The commandos had hardwired the bridge to destroy it.

When Guinness discovers the hidden wires, he sees that the bridge must be destroyed. Before he is shot, he pulls the switch and destroys the bridge. At the end, after the destruction, with soldiers dying, the last words of one of the engineers are, "Madness, sheer madness." Who would not agree that war is madness? The great powers of the time realized later that wars and empire building are a contradiction for human progress.

Gandhi (1982)

Produced by Richard Attenborough, the film is biographical about the world-famous Indian leader Mahatma Gandhi. Attenborough's particular inspiration was Gandhi's dictum, "It has always been a mystery to me how men can feel themselves honored by the humiliation of their fellow beings." Recall the advice of the ancient Indian sages not to judge and violate others.

The film was popular the world over; schools took students to see it for educational purposes, and it won eight academy awards, among others. The story is about Gandhi, a British-trained lawyer, who discovers that the British have made Indians second-class citizens in their own country. He fights for independence employing the technique of *Satyagraha*, meaning a path of truth and non-violence of thought and action. He took many vows including to always be truthful, and wore clothes similar to those of poor Indians. Imagine a freedom fighter with half of his body exposed, without weapons or violence, visiting England to meet aristocrats of the British government! No one could capture his life in a single film. I was an eyewitness to the freedom movement in its later years and to Gandhi's idealism; I had an opportunity to walk with him and spend a few hours when I was in my early teens.

Attenborough did a marvelous job producing and directing the film against many odds. Gandhi was a true "philosopher-king" as described by the ancient Indian sages, and fortunate to have the right nemesis in the British to be successful. Another of Gandhi's quotes reverberates with one of the ancients': "God and the devil both reside in our hearts," similar to the statement that good and evil are two opposites and cannot be separated.

One Flew Over the Cuckoo's Nest (1975)

The film is based on the novel by Ken Kesey, who had experience working in the California Veterans Hospital. Randle McMurphy, played by Jack Nicholson, is a fun-loving free-spirited crook who is sent to the state mental home for rehabilitation. The patients are under the watchful eye of the sadistic, tyrannical head nurse Ratched, played by Louise Fletcher. The environment in the mental home is such that a sane person would become insane.

There is plenty of psychic and somatic mixing in the story. Somatic sexual desires are considered a crime by the head nurse. The film shows how psychiatry makes patients drug-dependent. There is substantial evidence that psychic diseases cannot be totally cured with somatic medicine, and somatic needs cannot be suppressed by intellect or logic. Toward the end of the film, the doctors perform a lobotomy that makes McMurphy like a zombie. His friend Chief Bromden ends his misery in an act of mercy killing and escapes from "the cuckoo's nest." After seeing the movie, one would think twice about sending a loved one to such institutions. The film received five academy awards, including best film, best actor, and best actress.

City of God (2002)

The film is based on a true story about a housing project that was initiated in the 1960s in Rio de Janeiro for low-income people that degenerated into a violent, poverty-ridden, heart-breaking, savage slum of children. The dwellers of the slum are children making drugs and crime a way of life. The movie is also a study of the urban landscape from its illegitimate birth through its shocking maturity and, at the end, toward death.

The existence of these children is at the deepest level of the dark side of the somatic domain. There is hardly any morality, but it shows how children adapt to survive and become disconnected from the human traits of conscience, compassion, and hope. Only one child, Buscape, has inborn *Samskara* that prevents him from becoming a gangster, and his artistic talent leads him to become a celebrated photographer of his surroundings.

Forrest Gump (1994)

The film is about American history from the 1950s until the 1980s seen through the eyes of a simple, likable, but intellectually dull Forrest Gump, who has an IQ of 75. The character of Forest Gump is played superbly by Tom Hanks who won his second academy award for best actor in as many years. Forrest Gump, though mentally challenged, has the element of luck in his favor, and goes through the experience of significant events of the later part of the 20th century, meeting Presidents Kennedy, Johnson, and Nixon. He also becomes a Vietnam War hero by saving the life of his superior, Lieutenant Dan, who later helps him become wealthy in the shrimp business.

The film is a character study about how being honest, balanced, and having good character (*Samskara*) offers more than being intelligent. Intelligent Jenny, the love of Forrest Gump, gets deep into the American counterculture of drugs, alcohol, and war protestation. In the end, the *Samskaric* intuitive mind brings Forrest Gump prosperity and happiness while the mixed-up, unbalanced psyche brings Jenny misery and early death. However, Forrest is able to provide Jenny with the peaceful last days of her life. The film received many awards, including an academy award for best picture.

Butch Cassidy and the Sundance Kid (1969)

The black humor of Butch in the film comes out when he challenges Sundance about being fearful of drowning since he cannot swim. "What do you mean, you can't swim? The fall will probably kill you." They were about to jump from a great height into the river. If they did not jump, the Rangers chasing them would shoot them dead. It was foolish to think about drowning when death was certain, either by being shot or from the fall, just as it is foolish to be fearful of death to transcend. One has to die philosophically to transcend, and it was necessary for the two characters to "transcend" to escape the Rangers' bullets. Recall that transcendence toward the ultimate goal is the way against regression, just as a river flows toward its ultimate destination, the ocean.

Appendix 4
Insights from *The Celestine Prophecy* by James Redfield

The book is written as an adventure parable describing nine insights about human evolution and spiritual transformation as we enter the third millennium. The reason to include this section is because these insights are so close to the content of *Saving Us from Ourselves*, and the book was well-received in America in the 1990s.

The first insight ties us and everything we do with the spiritual sub-stratum, similar to *Atman* as the sub-stratum of every jiva (life) described in Advaita Vedanta.

The second insight is about our survival and well-being and that it is fine to take care of our needs, implying that we should take care of our somatic self.

The third and fourth insights are about energy and how we as individuals and organizations fight and steal from one another. There is a lot more energy in the universe that can support all of us, and there is no need to steal and go to war for it.

The fifth insight is about evolutionary processes and transcendence to higher levels of vibration. Regression stops evolution and one needs to work hard not to fall back into old habits.

The sixth insight is about intuition and how important it is to get guidance from our inner self, similar to the involution recommended by Sri Aurobindo. The writer even advocates integrating the truth of the West and the East for higher and purer truth. Enlightenment is obtained within and marked by peace of mind and detachment from worldly things. Progress is made not just by employing logic (intellect) but also other faculties, including intuition.

The seventh insight is about positive thinking, and prompts us to be observers of our own minds, as suggested by Krishnamurti. One needs to filter out the negative and put more emphasis on the positive. Recall the story of the Indian chief and the two dogs in his tent. It is a challenge sometimes in adverse situations to find a silver lining, but there is always one to be found.

The eighth insight warns strongly against attachment to something or someone, which can stop growth. It is like the Peter Principle in management, which states that one rises on a ladder of management to the level of one's incompetence. Here incompetence implies the weakness of being attached, which stops the upward movement. One needs to learn to disconnect and go forward.

The ninth insight envisions a mass migration of souls to the highest level of evolution. Centuries from now, everyone will know what their goal in life is. Everyone will be in pursuit of truth, naturally, and everyone will be in harmony within and with others. In the writer's words, "As humans, we will discover that we are the culmination of the whole of evolution. We are getting lighter [with great mental agility], with a high frequency of vibration. The highly evolved would then glow, crossing barriers from this life to the next. The conscious crossing over is a path shown by Christ and Yudhistir of the epic Mahabharata. Ultimately the meaning of death becomes obsolete."

Appendix 5
Mass Human Psychology and the Laws of Nature

The behaviors of crowds and individuals as well as organizations follow the laws of Nature. A crowd's behavior can, at first glance, seem chaotic, directionless, and without focus—somewhat like our own minds with random thoughts. Yet, just as a hurricane close up may appear to be a torrent of wind and rain, a satellite view from above shows it to be a circling mass of air and water following specific natural laws. It has a central "eye," rising and falling barometric zones, and a path that is determined by the warm and cold currents of water and air that created it. Human existence may seem directionless and chaotic, but time eventually reveals a "method to its madness." Markets of stocks, bonds and commodities similarly move to natural laws. They appear to mimic the directionless mass psychology of crowds, and follow certain laws that move them through intervals of "bulls" and "bears," that, seen from "above," have a logical pattern and even a natural order.

The laws of evolution and of demand and supply described in Chapter 4 are applicable to every level of human existence, including the rising and falling of markets. Markets are influenced by what wages are paid to workers; what workers pay for food, rent or mortgage; and where they travel. The pricing pattern of stocks in the short duration may resemble the erratic movement of fish in water, or perhaps the pattern of a chaotic electronic signal of an amplifier with no input signal. But with some insight and a new perspective on a stock, it may reveal a definite long-term pattern. Markets are always evolving and becoming better organized. The regulatory agencies tend to devise laws so that the catastrophic fluctuations and volatility of the market are minimized. However, neither Nature nor the market can be tamed by man totally and absolutely.

Markets, like Nature, are fractal, implying that they have self-similar patterns. The price chart patterns of Dow Jones Industrial are similar, regardless of the time coordinate, which could be in units of hours, days, weeks or months. The tree is an example in Nature, where the smallest branch resembles the largest. Another example is that of a sea-shore line—the patterns are self-similar, no matter from what height one observes the shoreline.

Market setbacks often seem to bring "death" to the market as it happened in 1987, 2000, 2002, and 2008. However with time, the market becomes "alive" again and functions as anticipated. It is amazing how the market has a capacity to become organized out of a chaotic situation. It seems to have the same attitude as many organizations made of various individuals with their own ideas, which eventually come together to create a cohesive whole. Sometimes chaos just needs time to come together. Orders of the world are created out of chaos. So too we see this with markets and organizations. We have observed how time heals almost all wounds, physical as well as mental. Destructive orders like tsunamis cause deep wounds or even death; creative orders support progress.

Let us consider some market clichés based on the laws of Nature:

1. What goes up comes down. This refers to the law of gravity and the law of demand and supply. If, for example, demand goes up for a product that just came on the market and the supply is not enough, the price of the product goes up. However as supply catches up with demand, which usually happens because suppliers will produce more to make more profits, then the price of a particular product stabilizes. In time, an "over-supply" will make the price go down.

2. There is absolutely no free lunch, not now or ever! Though some advertisements say that you get something for nothing, this is not true. One always gives something that is valuable to the advertiser. This is analogous to the laws of conservation of mass and energy. Mass or energy cannot be destroyed without accounting for it.

3. Growth engines run our economy. Often we hear that a particular sector—for example, information technology—is the "growth engine" of today's economy. Is there an engine in economy? The answer is actually "yes," because the economy can stall, accelerate or even overheat. Economies can even be "jump-started." So yes, the economy has many engines to make it move.

4. Markets gyrate between greed and fear, the two extremes of mass psychology. They are among the pairs of opposites discussed in Chapter 5. Our ancestors feared Nature due to ignorance of it. Ignorance is also the cause of fear and greed. Markets get oversold since fear overrules reason, causing indiscriminate selling and creating investment opportunities. Greed causes markets to be over-bought creating traps that lose money. Another similar cliché of the market is to buy low and sell high. Get in early at the ground level and get out when the price has gone to the stratosphere. But momentum players say, "Buy high and sell higher."

5. Hindsight is always 20/20, but markets are 80/20. It has been described extensively in Chapter 4, where Nature is described as 80/20.

6. One should not fight the Tape or the Fed. One should never go against the markets. Trend is your friend until it ends—ride the "waves" of the price movement. The trend is on track even if it is flat. Watch the slope and get off the slope if it drops like a rock. Do not stay too long if the trend becomes a tsunami. Do not ever think you have power over the waves. Get rid of arrogance and be humble to the market. Neither the market nor Nature is anyone's slave. One needs to remove the deadly foursome—hope, greed, vanity, and fear—to become a successful player.

7. Life is a game—so is playing the market. Contrary to what Einstein believed, God does play dice and God doesn't play favorites. Investors need to be emotionally detached but enjoy the ride of the market when it is climbing the wall of worries.

8. Money flows where it receives the best treatment. Money flows where it finds the best return with minimum risks. A superior return creates a force of attraction similar to a gravitational force. Money or capital is liquid and it flows whenever there is force or pressure applied to it. Capital, like power, is feminine, as was discussed in detail in Chapter 3. The feminine goddess Lakshmi in Indian tradition is the provider of wealth and material well-being.

9. Statistically Monday is the worst day of the week for selling. Recall that most heart attacks occur on Monday, mentioned in Chapter 3, due to mental conditioning.

10. The market resembles a pod of peas. The market is a Place where the Power to Pick and Purchase stocks will Produce Profits for Patient People. In the "pod of peas," one needs to consider companies providing indispensable goods with increasing profits.

11. No two bull markets are alike, since they are orders of different attributes. All bear markets resemble death and are similar to chaos.

12. There is no such thing as an absolutely safe investment, since Nature does not allow anything absolute and unchanging. We know that relativity rules in Nature and certainly it rules in the market. The high interest rates of over 15 percent were harmful to the U.S. economy in the 1980s; however, less than half of that rate busted the tech bubble in 2000.

13. The randomness of stock prices is comparable or similar to the random motion of air molecules.

14. The greater the randomness of the stock prices, the higher or lower the stock price could move and therefore the higher the premium (cost) of the stock options (puts and calls).

15. The high frequency trading is likely to become more common as stock exchanges get closer and closer to an automated system.

16. Trading frequency increases based upon relevant news. For example, more traders will buy the stock of an oil company after the announcement of a large oil discovery.

17. "All this works great, until it does not." Everything falls apart when a "Black Swan" event takes place, i.e. an event like a tsunami that exists at the farthest reaches of probability.

18. Attributes of "Black Swan" events include that it is unpredictable, it is an extremely rare event, and it is unquantifiable. It carries a massive impact wherever and whenever it occurs. Furthermore, after the event occurs and becomes history, scholars tend to make it predictable, i.e. scholars tend to bring it within the probability distribution curve, i.e. they tend to make a natural 80/20 "Black Swan" event into a 20/20 "White Swan" event.

19. A computer algorithm for stock trading is good until it fails to generate a profit. And in time, the lifespan of a trading algorithm will shorten and shorten.

20. Today, all markets are interconnected. Complexities of derivatives have linked markets together that would not normally be linked. A rise or drop in equity markets could cause the same effect in commodity markets. The correlation coefficient of one market with respect to another is never constant.

21. The knowledge of economics is imperfect and will remain imperfect since Nature and therefore human psychology will resist perfection.

Increasing successful tighter controls over markets should increase the agility and decrease fluctuations of the price movement. This is analogous to brain waves (EEG); an alert brain implies tighter control or having waves of higher frequencies and lower amplitude and vice versa.

There is interdependence between markets and other phenomena. For example, every dynamic system in Nature exchanges matter and energy to survive. Living organisms need food, water, and an air supply to exist and are self-organizing, meaning they choose their structure and function.

Markets function like living organisms. Just as blood in our systems nourishes all our cells and provides oxygen and energy, currency provides sustenance to the market and an economy. Excessive currency in circulation will create inflation, similar to excess blood in an obese human body. In an electrical system, voltage causes the current flow, similar to blood pressure, which causes the flow of blood. Likewise in an economy, the supply of goods and services is a type of "current" with "demand" being equivalent to electrical voltage—pumps, engines, batteries and demand are needed to create the flow. In a market economy, the price of goods is a form of resistance or regulator of the flow—a higher price causes less demand and a lower supply. Diversification of investment can help minimize risk, the same as eating diverse foods helps to maintain good health.

With a heart free of hatred, a mind free of worries and anxieties, live simply, love generously without conditions, give more, expect less, care deeply, speak kindly, and play the game of life without fear. We are players and the world is a stage—there is a moment to enter the stage, and a moment to depart. Stay active and involved. Participate without attachment. Remain nimble and agile. Then the game of life becomes rewarding.

Glossary

Advaita: Non-dualism

Aham: I, being self-centered, egotistic

Ahamkara: I-ness, arrogance

Ahimsa: Non-violence

Ajanta: Caves in central India, known for paintings

Anthropic: Pertaining to man's extremely unlikely existence, as if there were a supernatural design for man to observe and participate in

Artha: 1. Meaning; 2. Money

Ashrama: Four stages of the human lifespan

Atman: Human soul

Avidya: Knowledge of the Lower Order

Aum: Primal sound

Ayurveda: System of knowledge of physical and mental health

Bhagavad Gita: A poem within the epic, *Mahabharata*

Bijatma: Seed-Soul

Bindu: Drop, zero

Brahmacharya: First stage of human lifespan *(See Ashrama)*

Brahman: Supreme Reality

Burkha: Head-covering garment worn by orthodox Muslim women

Chatur, Chatuh: Four

Correlation coefficient: The degree by which two variables are linked.

Complementarity: Condition of being complementary to something

Daan: Charitable

Daman: Control over desires

Dana: Charity

Daya: Compassion

Dehatma: Soul of the physical body

Dharma: Moral and ethical duty

EEG: Electroencephalogram. A test that measures the electrical activity of the brain, produced by neurons, as recorded by an electroencephalograph. Used as a diagnostic tool.

Ekal Vidyalaya: *Ekal*=single; *Vidyalaya*=school; a place of learning

Ellora: Caves in central India, known for their sculptures

Empirical self: Total human self containing somatic, psychic and spiritual selves

Ganesha: A deity worshipped at the beginning of events; son of Shiva and Parvati

Gita: See *Bhagavad Gita*

Grahastha: Householder; second of the four stages of the human lifespan *(See Ashrama)*

Gyan yoga: Path or yoga of knowledge

Gyanatma: Knowledge-Soul; knowing soul

Jaina: Follower of Mahavira

Janaka: A King, father of Sita in the epic, *Ramayana*

Jataka: 1. Someone born; 2. Buddhist stories

Jivatma: Soul as individual life force; soul in bondage

Kama: God of love; Eros

Kundalini: In yoga, the primary energy, lying coiled and dormant at the base of the spinal cord

Lakshmi: Wealth. Consort of Vishnu, the God of Sustenance

Leela: Play; game of life

Lobhayati: Greed-causing

Mahabharata, the epic

Mahavira: Founder of Jainism; 24th Tirthankara; literally, "Great Courageous One"

Mandala: In yoga, a circle of symbolic value

Maya: In Vedanta, the prime illusion

Moksha: Liberation

Morphic field: A system of self-transmitting information

Nagarjuna: A Buddhist sage

Nirguna: Free from all qualities; Brahman without any qualities. *(See Saguna)*

Paramatma: Supreme Soul

Pardah: Veil worn by orthodox Muslim women

Patanjali: An ancient sage, philosopher

Pratham: First

Prematma: Loving soul

Pancha sheela: Five good behaviors in Buddhism

Purushartha: Four major efforts in human life: *Dharma, Artha, Kama* and *Moksha*

Quaternites: Karl Jung's four elements of psychology

Ramanuja: A philosopher and teacher

Rishis: Ancient sages

Ruta: Cosmic order; material form of Brahman accessible to senses by cultivating *Samskara*; Nature in its best mood, benevolent, loving, and truthful; first evolute of Nature

Saguna: Having Brahman-possessing qualities *(See Nirguna)*

Sakshi: Witness

Samskara: Culturing spontaneous physical impulses and reflexes of the pre-psyche within the somatic self; positive, life-fulfilling spontaneities; integration of opposites through the experience of the nerves of the body

Satyagraha: Truth force; a term central to Mahatma Gandhi's thought and action

Shakti, Shakta: Literally, "Power"; by extension "Supreme Feminine Deity"; *Shakta*: worshipper of supreme feminine deity

Shanti: Peace

Saraswati: Goddess of learning

Sat-chit-ananda: Being-Knowing-Bliss

Shankara: A philosopher; founder of the Kevaladvaita School

Sub-ration: Rating the level below par; rejection of the stuff of lower
values, and exploration of the stuff of higher values

Sunyata: Shunyata: Nothingness (zero); similar to Nirguna Brahman

Sutratma: Soul as thread; a threading and integrating soul

Swadhyaya parivar: A cultural-religious movement in the second half of
the 20th century in western India

Upanishad: Literally "to sit close to" a teacher; generic name given to
the ancient Indian works of philosophy

Vanaprastha: Third stage of human lifespan *(See Ashrama)*

Vedanta: Literally "the end or culmination of the Vedas"; also a system
of Indian philosophy

Vipassana: In Buddhist tradition, a mode of contemplation

Yatra: Journey, pilgrimage

Yudhister: A character in Indian mythology. The oldest brother of five
in the *Tale of Ma Bharata*. Considered to be a very honest man who
never told a single lie.

Bibliography

Batra, Ravi. *Greenspan's Fraud*. New York, Palgrave Macmillan, 2005.

Batra, Ravi. *The Great American Deception*. New York, John Wiley & Sons, 1996.

Bernstein, Peter, I. *Capital Ideas*. New York, The Free Press, a division of Macmillan, 1992.

Black, John. *Oxford Dictionary of Economics*. Oxford and New York, Oxford University Press, 1997, 2002.

Campbell, Joseph. *The Power of Myth*. Conversation with Bill Moyers presented by PBS, distributed at PBS Store and by Mystic Fire Video, Inc., New York. Broadcast in 1994.

Capra, Fritjof. *The Tao of Physics*. Boulder, Shambhala Publications, 1983.

Capra, Fritjof. *Lectures. The New Vision of Reality*. Bombay, Bharatiya Vidya Bhavan, 1983.

Chopra, Deepak. *The Seven Spiritual Laws of Success*. San Rafael, Amber-Allen Publishing, 1994.

Chopra, Deepak. Tapes on different subjects including Quantum Healing.

Desai, Mahdev. *Gandhi [in Ceylon]*. Madras, S. Ganesan, Triplicane, 1928.

Deutsch, Eliot. *Advaita Vedanta*. Honolulu, East-West Center Press, 1969, 1973.

Durant, Will. *The Story of Civilization, Our Oriental Heritage*. New York, MJF Books, 1935, 1963.

Goswami, Amit. *The Self-Aware Universe*. New York, G. P. Putnam's Sons, 1993, 1995.

Great Thinkers of the Eastern World. I. P. McGreal, editor. New York, HarperCollins, 1995.

Greenstein, George. *The Symbiotic Universe*. New York, William Morrow and Company, Inc., 1988.

Hamer, Dean. *The God Gene: How Faith Is Hardwired into Our Genes*. New York, Doubleday, 2004.

Hanh, Thich Nhat. *Living Buddha, Living Christ*. New York, Riverhead Books, Putnam & Sons, 1995.

Hawking, Stephen. *A Brief History of Time*. Toronto and New York, Bantam Books, 1988.

Jitatmananda, Swami. *Holistic Science and Vedanta*. Bombay, Bharatiya Vidya Bhavan, 1991.

Jung, C. G. "A Psychical Approach to the Dogma of the Trinity." 1942. In *Collected Works, Vol. II*.

Koch, Richard. *The 80/20 Principle*. New York, Doubleday, 1998.

Kothari, D. S. *Atom and Self*. Bombay, Bharatiya Vidya Bhavan, 1983.

Krishnamurti, J. Audiotapes and videotapes. KFA, PO Box 1560, Ojai, CA 93024. www.kfa.org

Krishnamurti, J. *The Book of Life*. R. E. Mark Lee, editor. San Francisco, HarperCollins, 1995.

Kuhn, Thomas. *The Structure of Scientific Revolution*. Chicago, University of Chicago Press, 1996.

Kumar, Nirmal. *The Tao of Psychology*. Bombay, Bharatiya Vidya Bhavan, 1993.

Mandelbrot, Benoit, and Richard Hudson. *The (Mis) Behavior of Markets*. New York, Basic Books, 2004.

McEvilley, Thomas. *The Shape of Ancient Thought*. New York, Allworth Press, 2002.

Murchie, Guy. *The Seven Mysteries of Life*. Boston, Houghton Mifflin Company, 1978.

Okasha, Samir. *Philosophy of Science*. Oxford, UK, Oxford University Press, 2002.

Paine, Jeffery. *Father India*. New York, HarperCollins, 1998.

Parekh, Bhikhu. *Gandhi*. Oxford, UK, Oxford University Press, 1997.

Paz, Octavio. *Lights of India*. San Diego and New York, Harcourt Brace and Company, 1995.

Prigogine, Ilya, and Isabelle Stengers. *Order out of Chaos*. London, Fontana and Bantam Books, 1984, 1985, 1988.

Reese, W. L. *Dictionary of Philosophy and Religion*. New Jersey, Humanities Press; and Sussex, Harvester Press, 1980.

Redfield, James. *The Celestine Prophecy*. New York, Warner Books, 1993.

Rucker, Rudy. *Mind Tools*. Boston, Houghton Mifflin Company, 1987.

Sheldrake, Rupert. *The Presence of the Past*. London, Park Street Press, 1995.

Tharoor, Shashi. *Nehru*. New York, Arcade Publishing, 2003.

The Yoga Sutras of Patanjali. Christopher Chapple translator. Bombay and New York, Sri Satguru Publications, 1990.

About the Author

Navin Doshi is an engineer, philosopher, philanthropist, and astute trader in financial asset management. Originally from the Gurjarat, India, his parents later migrated to Bombay (now Mumbai). As a young boy of nine in Bombay, Doshi shared a walk with Mahatma Gandhi during a visit to Mahabelshver with his parents. In 1958 Mr. Doshi came to the United States for a post-graduate program in engineering, first at the University of Michigan, then at University of California at Los Angeles (UCLA).

During his career as an aerospace engineer, he was the recipient of NASA awards and U.S. patents. Mr. Doshi and his wife, Pratima, are the parents of two children and the proud grandparents of six children. They currently own and manage residential income properties, including mobile home parks in California. In 1999, Mr. and Mrs. Doshi endowed the Doshi Chair of Indian History at UCLA, and he has been active as a fund raiser and consultant on numerous projects that particularly deal with education, culture, tradition, history, and archaeology. The Doshis are founding members and the contributors for the establishment of the prestigious Sarder Patel Award at UCLA for exceptional doctoral dissertations in the field of Indian culture and history. The Doshis have also endowed a professorship at Loyola Marymount University, occupied by Dr. Christopher Chapple, a highly recognized scholar of Indic traditions, who also administers the Doshi Bridge Builder Award ($10,000) Program. Recipient of numerous honors from his Alma Maters in India and in the US, Mr. Doshi writes articles on investment and philosophy for local media. The articles are available at www.nalandainternational.org.

INDEX